STUDY G

Steven Ross

EDUCATIONAL PSYCHOLOGY

Theory into Practice

SECOND EDITION

Robert E. Slavin

Johns Hopkins University

PRENTICE HALL
Englewood Cliffs, New Jersey 07632

Printed in the United States of America

10 9 8 7 6 5 4 3 2 1

0-13-236894-3

Prentice-Hall International (UK) Limited, London
Prentice-Hall of Australia Pty. Limited, Sydney
Prentice-Hall Canada Inc., Toronto
Prentice-Hall Hispanoamericana, S.A., Mexico
Prentice-Hall of India Private Limited, New Delhi
Prentice-Hall of Japan, Inc., Tokyo
Simon & Schuster Asia Pte. Ltd., Singapore
Editora Prentice-Hall do Brasil, Ltda., Rio de Janeiro

Contents

Preface

The purpose of the Study Guide is to help you learn important facts, terms, and concepts from EDUCATIONAL PSYCHOLOGY by R. Slavin (2nd edition). Keep in mind that using the "Guide" without reading the corresponding chapters in EDUCATIONAL PSYCHOLOGY will not be very beneficial. That is because the Guide does not teach new material; rather, it reinforces what your text has taught by reviewing important content and testing your learning through a variety of quiz items and special exercises. Some "tips" for using the Guide will be provided shortly. First, let's become acquainted with its features.

Contents

The Guide is organized into 15 chapters corresponding to those in the textbook. Each chapter contains the following sections:

1. Chapter Outline. This section provides a detailed summary of chapter content, listing the major sections and subsections of the text, along with descriptions of each. The Chapter Outline should prove helpful for both overviewing topics before beginning a chapter and reviewing what was covered after the chapter has been studied.

2. Chapter Objectives. This section lists the learning objectives for the chapter. It therefore tells you the types of knowledge and performance skills you should have acquired when you complete the chapter.

3. Matching Warm-Ups. This section contains a series of matching quizzes intended to get you mentally ready for your chapter review. Most of the quizzes contain related terms that are easy to confuse; others called "notable names" help you to relate important contributors (to theory and research) to their contributions.

4. Key Terms. This section contains a listing of the "key concepts" introduced in the chapter, followed by completion items that incorporate those terms. The list includes only those terms that appear in bold type (with special marginal definitions) in the text.

5. Completion Questions. This quiz section tests your recall of important chapter content. Some items are "retests" of the key terms reviewed in Section 4, whereas others concern additional terminology, names of people, outcomes of research, components of theories and models, and more.

6. Multiple-Choice. This quiz section contains a comprehensive set of 20 multiple-choice questions that test factual as well as conceptual knowledge. Completing it should provide excellent practice for multiple-choice exams.

7. Applications. These exercises require you to apply what you have learned in the context of new problems, simulations of school events, and research demonstrations. When you "experience" principles and methods in this manner, they will become much more meaningful and real to you compared to just reading about their uses in the text. Certain chapters include an application from the EDUCATIONAL PSYCHOLOGY COMPUTER DISK, an additional supplement for your text. If you have access to the disk, the computer exercises should provide interesting and involving ways of practicing the applications covered (e.g., Piagetian interviews, grading, testing, Student Teams-Achievement Divisions, and more).

8. Essay/Discussion Questions. This section presents open-ended questions that test your knowledge and understanding of important issues and practices in theory and research. These should provide helpful preparation for essay exams or class discussions.

9. Answers. This section contains answers to the objective questions presented in previous sections. Textbook pages containing the information needed to answer the questions are identified by number to the right of the correct answers.

How to Use the Guide

Everyone's learning style and study habits are different. Thus, you are probably the best judge of how to make the Guide work most effectively for you. Some recommendations to stimulate your thinking as are follows:

1. Before reading a chapter, examine the Chapter Outline (Section 1) to obtain an overview of the material. Carefully review the Chapter Objectives (Section 2), since these tell you what you are expected to know when you complete the chapter. Scan some of the practice items (especially "key terms"), but now is not the time to test yourself--read the chapter first.

2. Read/study the chapter (consider using the SQ4R study method described in the text).

3. Review the Chapter Outline and Chapter Objectives to make sure that major topics are familiar and that you have learned what is expected (Sections 1 and 2).

4. Complete the Matching Warm-Ups first (Section 3). If you find yourself confusing the terms or not recognizing them, you probably need to review the text. If you perform reasonably well (above 80% correct) proceed with the next section. Complete the sections in order of their presentation, since they are purposely arranged to progress from simpler types of learning (facts, terms) to higher-order learning (applications, analysis, synthesis).

5. Complete Application exercises by yourself or in a study group (Section 7).

6. Write or orally present answers to the Discussion questions (Section 8).

7. Reread the text, concentrating on any areas on which quiz performances were low.

8. Get a good night's sleep, and hope that your instructor also had a good sleep the night <u>before</u> he/she constructed the test.

Educational psychology can be a fascinating and highly useful subject for teachers. It is hoped that use of this Study Guide will help to make your learning experiences in this area both more rewarding and more enjoyable.

1 Educational Psychology: A Tool for Teachers

CHAPTER OUTLINE

I. What Makes a Good Teacher
   A. Subject matter knowledge
      1. Must know one's subject
      2. Must know how to transmit that subject
   B. Instruction
      1. Pedagogy--the link between what is planned and what is actually learned
      2. Positive characteristics and effective practices lead to good teaching

II. Why This Book Was Written
   A. Educational psychology: A problem-solving approach
      1. The focus of educational psychology
      2. Drawing on successful practices to isolate strategies that work
   B. Teachers on teaching: Learning to teach

III. Why is Research in Educational Psychology Important?
   A. What good is research in educational psychology to the teacher?
      1. Testing of theories
      2. Information on developmental patterns
      3. Identification of effective methods for discipline

B. Research methods in educational psychology
   1. Experiments
   2. Laboratory experiment
   3. Randomized field experiments
      a. Experimental group
      b. Control group
   4. Single-case experiments
   5. Correlational studies
      a. Positive correlation
      b. Negative correlation
      c. Uncorrelated variables
      d. Correlation coefficients
   6. Descriptive research
      a. Survey or interview
      b. Ethnography

IV. Why Teaching is the Hardest Job in the World and Why Teachers Secretly Love It--A Dedication

Summary/Study Questions/Suggested Readings

CHAPTER OBJECTIVES

1. List the major questions that educational psychologists try to answer.
2. Cite at least one commonly held belief about teaching that educational psychologists have proved wrong.
3. Explain how theories you hold about behavior and learning will influence how you try to solve problems in the classroom.
4. Describe several types of experiments used to understand learning.
5. Describe the difference between a correlational relationship and a causal relationship.
6. Analyze an experiment and judge whether its results can be applied in the classroom.

MATCHING WARM-UPS

Match the letters of the descriptions on the right to the corresponding items on the left. A given item from the right column may be used more than once or not at all.

Quiz 1: Products of Research

_____ a. Law	1. A thoroughly tested explanation of the relationship between factors
_____ b. Principle	2. A null hypothesis for a study
_____ c. Theory	3. A broad explanation of learning
	4. An explanation of how factors relate

Quiz 2: Types of Research

_____ a. Laboratory study
_____ b. Single-case experiment
_____ c. Randomized field experiment
_____ d. Correlational study
_____ e. Descriptive research

1. A survey, for example
2. The relationship between two variables
3. Does not involve quantification
4. Higher external validity; lower internal validity
5. Involves repeated observations
6. Higher internal validity; lower external validity

Quiz 3: Correlation Results

_____ a. Positive correlation
_____ b. Negative correlation
_____ c. Zero correlation

1. High scores on one variable are associated with low scores on the other
2. Scores on one variable are unrelated to scores on the other
3. High scores on one variable are associated with high scores on the other

KEY TERMS

Fill in the blanks below with the letters identifying the following concepts. Each concept is used one time only.

A. Educational psychology
B. Pedagogy
C. Principle
D. Law
E. Theory
F. Treatments
G. Variable
H. Experiment
I. Random assignment
J. Laboratory experiments
K. Internal validity
L. Randomized field experiments
M. Experimental group
N. Control group
O. External validity
P. Single-case experiment
Q. Correlational study
R. Positive correlation
S. Negative correlation
T. Uncorrelated
U. Correlation coefficients
V. Descriptive research

1. "Methods of instruction" that provide a link between what the teacher wants students to learn and students' actual learning are called _____.

2. Something that can have more than one value such as height, test scores, and age is called a(n) _____.

3. _____ is the degree to which experimental results are due to treatment effects rather than to extraneous factors.

4. _____ is the study of the processes through which learning and teaching take place in school and non-school settings.

5. _____ is a procedure designed to establish equality of treatment groups by determining selection of subjects (participants) according to chance.

6. By being conducted in artificial but highly structured settings, _____ increase degree of control over treatments.

7. Experimental research typically involves comparison of a(n) _____ which receives a special treatment to a(n) _____ which does not receive that treatment.

8. Two variables are said to be _____ when there is no relationship between them.

9. The examination of relationships between variables as they naturally occur is the focus of a(n) _____.

10. A principle that has been thoroughly tested is called a(n) _____.

11. A set of related principles and laws that explains broad aspects of learning is a(n) _____.

12. Experiments in educational psychology often involve the administration of different _____ to test their effectiveness for learning.

13. _____, which can range from -1 to +1, indicate the degree of relationship between two or more variables.

14. Studies in which treatments are applied to one individual or group to determine changes in behavior over time are called _____.

15. The degree to which experimental results are applicable to real-life settings is defined as _____.

16. A research orientation used to test the effectiveness of different treatments is _____.

17. Two variables are said to have a(n) _____ when high scores on one tend to be associated with high scores on the other.

18. An explanation of the relationship between factors such as reinforcement and attitude is called a(n) _____.

19. _____ involves observing and relating events of interest without attempt to manipulate or influence any environmental properties.

20. Two variables are said to have a(n) _____ when high scores on one tend to be associated with low scores on the other.

21. The random assignment of participants to treatments implemented under realistic conditions occurs in _____.

COMPLETION QUESTIONS

1. _____ refers to the methods of instruction used to promote learning.

2. Educational psychology is the study of learning, learners, and _____.

3. Individual principles that have been thoroughly tested are _____, whereas sets of related principles that explain more general phenomena are _____.

4. Special conditions or strategies that are examined in experiments are called _____.

5. A procedure that gives all individuals an equal chance of being placed in any treatment group is _____ assignment.

6. _____ is likely to increase as the realism of experimental treatments and conditions increase; _____ is likely to increase with greater control and structure in administering treatments.

7. Similar to the laboratory experiment, the _____ experiment involves random assignment of subjects to treatments, but the setting in which the research takes place is much more realistic.

8. In an experiment on the effects of different schedules of reinforcement, the group of subjects that does not receive a special reinforcement schedule would be called the _____ group.

9. Although the _____ experiment is effective for detecting pre- to post-treatment changes, one of its disadvantages is the need for frequent testing.

10. A researcher who measures students' math achievement scores and verbal achievement scores for the purpose of determining their relationship is conducting a _____ study.

11. If students who frequently misbehave tend to receive low school grades, one could infer that the relationship between frequency of misbehavior and school grades is _____.

12. The correlation between age and height for elementary school children would be _____.

13. Correlation coefficients range from _____ to _____.

14. A correlation coefficient of _____ indicates that the variables concerned are completely uncorrelated.

15. Two examples of _____ research are the survey and the ethnography.

MULTIPLE-CHOICE

Select the best answer for each of the following items.

1. Which of the following statements about theories is correct?

   a. A theory is based on clearly established and accepted outcomes, and thus is rarely refined once it gains acceptance.
   b. A theory integrates sets of related principles to explain broad aspects of learning.
   c. A theory tends to be narrower and more restrictive than a law.
   d. A theory is a prediction or hypothesis regarding the effects of certain variables.

2. A government agency requests that research be performed on the four topics listed below. Which one would probably least interest an educational psychologist?

   a. The causes of anxiety and neurosis in children
   b. Whether cooperative learning is more effective than individualized learning
   c. How cognitive and physical abilities change from age 1 to 18
   d. How rote memory can be improved

3. Which of the following is an example of random assignment?

   a. Boys are placed into one treatment group and girls into another.
   b. Out of 20 students who volunteer to be in a particular treatment group, 10 are selected by drawing numbers from a hat; the second group is then selected in the same way from the non-volunteer group.
   c. The first half of the class that enters the classroom are assigned to one treatment group, the remainder are assigned to the other group.
   d. None of the above.

4. Mrs. Lupfer is interested in comparing the effectiveness of two methods of teaching reading. She uses the first method with her morning class and the second with her afternoon class. She then compares the two classes on reading skills at the end of the year. Given only this information, which of the following conclusions can be made about Mrs. Lupfer's research?

   a. It has high internal validity.
   b. It is a properly conducted randomized field experiment.
   c. It has high external validity.
   d. None of the above.

5. External validity can be described as

   a. likely to increase with greater experimental control.
   b. usually lower in randomized field experiments than in laboratory experiments.
   c. not as important for researchers to consider as is internal validity.
   d. the degree to which results are relevant to real-life conditions.

6. A researcher visits Mr. Forrest's biology class daily over a three-week period. Her interest is to count and analyze changes in the number of questions that students ask the teacher on days prior to and following the showing of a film entitled "Ask Your Instructor: The Key to Learning." What type of research is being performed?

   a. Laboratory experiment
   b. Randomized field experiment
   c. Single-case experiment
   d. Correlation

7. A disadvantage of the single-case experiment is it

   a. is limited to individual students.
   b. is limited to outcomes that can be frequently measured.
   c. can be conducted only in laboratory settings
   d. takes more time to complete than do randomized field experiments.

8. A study in which the researcher closely observes children over a period of time and writes notes about their developmental growth represents a

   a. laboratory study.
   b. randomized field experiment.
   c. single-case experiment.
   d. descriptive study.

9. An ethnography is an example of a

   a. laboratory experiment.
   b. randomized field experiment.
   c. single-case experiment.
   d. descriptive study.

10. A college professor compares two methods of teaching math to children by visiting a local school and randomly assigning sixth-graders to an experimental treatment that emphasizes meaningful word problems and a control treatment that emphasizes abstract word problems. Following the lessons, which take about an hour to administer, students are individually tested for learning in a vacant classroom, using assessment materials prepared by the professor. This research is an example of a

   a. laboratory experiment.
   b. randomized field experiment.
   c. single-case experiment.
   d. correlational study.

11. A researcher is interested in determining whether children who watch a great deal of night-time TV tend to act more aggressively in school than others. The research method he uses involves collecting scores on both variables from each student in a class of 30 and determining their degree of relationship. This research is an example of a

   a. laboratory experiment.
   b. randomized field experiment.
   c. single-case experiment.
   d. correlational study.

12. Probably the most frequently used research method in educational psychology is the

   a. correlational study.
   b. ethnography.
   c. laboratory study.
   d. randomized field experiment.

13. Which of the following correlation coefficients indicates the weakest degree of relationship between the variables concerned?

   a. .08
   b. .68
   c. -.15
   d. .55

14. Which of the following correlation coefficients indicates the strongest degree of relationship between the variables concerned?

a. -.84
b. .65
c. .40
d. .00

15. The correlation between mathematics grades and English grades in school would probably be

a. positive.
b. negative.
c. close to zero.

16. The correlation between height and acting ability is likely to be

a. positive.
b. negative.
c. close to zero.

17. The correlation between height and weight for elementary school children is likely to be

a. positive.
b. negative.
c. close to zero.

18. The correlation between number of absences and grades for tenth-grade English students is likely to be

a. positive.
b. negative.
c. close to zero.

19. A guidance counselor suspects that children who are the most popular in her school tend to use profanity the least. The type of correlation she is predicting is

a. positive.
b. negative.
c. close to zero.

20. Suppose that predictions of the guidance counselor in item 19 were correct. On the basis of the study, what could she safely conclude?

a. Usage of profanity and popularity are related.
b. Usage of profanity reduces popularity.
c. Usage of profanity increases popularity.
d. Increased popularity reduces usage of profanity.

APPLICATION: "Playing" Educational Psychologist

Based on your knowledge and intuitions about learning, see if you can derive your own "theories" about each of the practices listed below. Do you feel that the practice is effective for learning? If so, how? Which type of student is most likely to benefit?

A. Grouping students according to ability in teaching elementary school math.

B. Encouraging students to take notes during lectures.

C. Establishing cooperative learning situations in which students learn in groups to maximize overall team scores.

D. Frequently reinforcing (praising) correct responses.

E. Giving public reprimands for improper behaviors.

F. Frequently questioning students during lecture presentations.

G. Establishing competitive grading situations in which students are evaluated in comparison to one another.

H. Using physical punishment when students misbehave.

I. Placing handicapped children in regular classes as opposed to special education classes as much as possible.

APPLICATION: Research Methods

Ms. Gleason, a junior high school principal, believes that parental involvement with children's schoolwork can raise achievement by providing both a positive model and a source of assistance on difficult learning tasks. To test this, she obtains a list of parents who are active members of the PTA and have a child in the eighth grade. She then sends each parent a special set of instructions and tutoring packet. Included in the packet are special drill exercises on various rules (e.g., multiplying fractions, exponents) taught during the year. The instructions provide direction for encouraging the completion of homework, providing tutorial assistance, and administering the drill exercises. The other parents of sixth-graders do not receive any special materials or communications from the principal's office.

At the end of the year, Ms. Gleason has all sixth-graders take a comprehensive math test on the year's work. She then compares the performances of children whose parents received the "parental involvement" materials with those of children whose parents did not receive the special materials. The respective group averages are 88.3% and 77.8%, which are determined by statistical methods to be significantly different. Ms. Gleason concludes that "parental involvement with children's schoolwork in mathematics facilitates performance." She is naturally very pleased by this result and spends the afternoon celebrating at her favorite bakery.

React to Ms. Gleason's research with regard to the following questions:

A. What type of research had Ms. Gleason apparently planned to perform (laboratory experiment, randomized field experiment, correlation, single-case, descriptive)? What attributes of the study lead you to make this choice?

B. Did there appear to be an experimental group and control group? If so, identify them.

C. Did Ms. Gleason actually succeed in conducting the type of study you identified in #1? Explain your answer.

D. Does the internal validity of the study appear high? Explain your answer.

E. Does the external validity of the study appear high? Explain your answer.

F. Is the conclusion reached justified? If so, explain the basis of support. If not, what alternative conclusion appears more justified?

G. What improvements, if any, might be made to strengthen the design?

<u>APPLICATION:</u> Correlational Studies

A researcher collects scores from high school males on the following variables: popularity (from a questionnaire), athletic ability (ratings from the physical education teachers), math achievement, English achievement, and number of bad conduct marks on report cards during the year. Each variable is correlated with all other scores. Results are shown as follows:

	Athletic Ability	Math Achvemt.	English Achvemt.	Bad Conduct Marks
Popularity	.45	-.30	-.25	.15
Athletic Ability		-.10	.05	.15
Math Achievement			.83	-.40
English Achievement				-.32

A. Which two variables have the strongest relationship?

B. Which two have the weakest relationship?

C. For the group overall, as popularity increases, English achievement tends to _____.

D. For the group overall, as bad conduct marks increase, math achievement tends to _____.

E. As math achievement increases, English achievement tends to _____.

F. On the basis of this study, would it be valid to infer that high athletic ability causes high popularity? Explain your answer.

APPLICATION: Causal Cautions with Correlations

A. An elementary school teacher measures the left foot length and spelling achievement of every student in Grades 1-6. To her surprise, she obtains a significant positive correlation between these variables. Can she conclude that left foot length causes good spelling skills? Can she conclude that good spelling causes longer feet? If you disagree with both of these interpretations, what explanation do you feel is more valid?

B. A researcher counts the number of bars and number of churches in each of 300 randomly selected cities in the United States. To his shock, he finds that these two variables are positively correlated. Do bars cause churches (maybe a need to repent after drinking)? Do churches cause bars? If neither of these conclusions seem appropriate, to what factor do you attribute the relationship?

COMPUTER EXERCISE: Research

The EDUCATIONAL PSYCHOLOGY COMPUTER DISK for your text contains an exercise called FREE RECALL. The exercise tests memory abilities by presenting 20 items, one at a time, and asking the learner to recall all that he/she can remember. The program allows the following conditions to be varied:

A. Type of item (concrete words, abstract words, nonsense syllables)
B. Length of individual item exposure interval (1 second, 3 seconds, or 5 seconds)
C. Position of item in list (beginning one-third, middle one-third, last one-third)

Use the program to conduct a "laboratory exponent" that investigates the effects on recall of either of the above variables. Recommended steps involve:

1. Selecting one of the variables to study. (This part is easy!)
2. Formulating one or more hypotheses regarding the effects of that variable on learning.
3. Selecting a sample of people (e.g., classmates, children) and randomly assigning them to treatment groups (e.g., concrete vs. abstract vs. nonsense). Note: Should you decide to investigate the "item position" variable, you will need only one group, because each subject will be tested on recalling items in all three positions (beginning, middle, and end). In the case of the two other

variables, each subject will receive one condition only. In a real experiment you would probably want to test at least 10 people per group; you could use less for this exercise, but results will be less reliable.

4. Testing subjects in the respective treatments and recording the results (e.g., number of items recalled).
5. Analyzing the results and presenting conclusions. Did the conditions appear to produce different results? Was the nature of the differences (or lack of them) consistent with your hypotheses? Explain.

ESSAY/DISCUSSION

1. Describe what you believe are the characteristics and abilities of good teachers. If you were a principal interviewing candidates for an opening in your teaching area, which of those characteristics would you look for first? Explain why.

2. The choice between research methods depends upon numerous factors including the purposes of the study, resources available, and constraints of data collection conditions. Briefly describe each of the following methods and discuss what you believe to be its major advantages and disadvantages. Which method or methods seem most reasonable for teachers who are interested in conducting informal studies of teaching and learning variables? Explain. Choices: laboratory experiment, randomized field experiment, correlation, single-case study, descriptive study.

3. Suppose that you are interested in the relationship between note-taking and retention of subject matter presented in a lecture. Describe how you might investigate this question using (a) an experimental (either laboratory or field) design and (b) correlational design.

4. Define and differentiate between internal and external validity. What types of conditions help to foster each? Can both types of validity be high in a single study or is it necessarily the case that as one increases, the other decreases? Explain.

ANSWERS

Matching Warm-Ups

Quiz 1	Quiz 2	Quiz 3
a. 1 (5)	a. 6 (9)	a. 3 (11)
b. 4 (5)	b. 5 (11)	b. 1 (11)
c. 3 (5)	c. 4 (9)	c. 2 (11)
	d. 2 (11)	
	e. 1 (13)	

Key Terms

1.	B (3)	8.	T (11)	15.	O (10)
2.	G (8)	9.	Q (11)	16.	H (8)
3.	K (9)	10.	D (5)	17.	R (11)
4.	A (3)	11.	E (5)	18.	C (5)
5.	I (8)	12.	F (8)	19.	V (13)
6.	J (9)	13.	U (12)	20.	S (11)
7.	M,N (9)	14.	P (10)	21.	L (9)

Completion Questions

1. pedagogy (3)
2. teaching (3)
3. laws; theories (5)
4. treatments (8)
5. random (8)
6. external validity; internal validity (8,9)
7. randomized field (9)
8. control (9)
9. single-case (11)
10. correlational (11)
11. negative (11)
12. positive (11)
13. -1.00; +1.00 (12)
14. 0 (12)
15. descriptive (13)

Multiple-choice

1.	b (5)	6.	c (10-11)	11.	d (11)	16.	c (11-12)
2.	a (3)	7.	b (11)	12.	a (11)	17.	a (11-12)
3.	d (8)	8.	d (13)	13.	a (12)	18.	b (11-12)
4.	d (8-10)	9.	d (13)	14.	a (12)	19.	b (11-12)
5.	d (10)	10.	a (10)	15.	a (11-12)	20.	a (12)

Application: Research Methods

A. Randomized-field experiment. She is manipulating the parental involvement variable using real-life learning materials and conditions.

B. Experimental: Children of parental involvement group
Control: Children of other parents (not receiving special materials)

C. She made a critical error by failing to randomly assign subjects to treatments. The PTA parents are likely to be more active and concerned than other parents. Thus, the experimental group may have an advantage before the treatments are even administered.

D. Internal validity is extremely low: (a) sample is biased; and (b) experimental group not only experienced parental involvement, they also received extra drill and practice! Thus, it will be impossible to isolate treatment (parental involvement) effects from sampling and practice variables.

E. With improvements in the methods external validity could be high. The materials and procedures used by parents, the math lessons studied, learning conditions, and posttesting are all realistic and seemingly quite feasible to use in real-life programs.

F. The conclusion reached is not justified. All one can conclude is that children of PTA members who receive special parental involvement and additional drill and practice perform better on a mathematics achievement test than children whose parents are not PTA members and do not receive these special interventions.

G. The main improvements would be to (a) randomly assign children and their parents to conditions and (b) restrict the parental involvement variable to support and motivational activities that do not involve additional teaching.

Application: Correlational Studies

A. math achievement and English achievement
B. athletic ability and English achievement
C. decrease
D. decrease
E. increase
F. no; it can be concluded that high athletic ability is associated with high popularity. It is not necessarily the case that the relationship is causal. Athletic ability may be associated with other variables (membership in high prestige social groups) that have more direct influences on popularity.

2 Theories of Development

CHAPTER OUTLINE

I. Aspects of Development
   A. Continuous and discontinuous theories
      1. Continuous theories assume a smooth developmental progression
      2. Discontinuous theories or "stage theories" emphasize the uneven steps in developmental progression
   B. The stages
      1. Sensorimotor stage (birth to two years)
         a. Initially governed by reflexes
         b. Intentional behavior emerges next
         c. Object permanence develops
         d. Trial-and-error learning
         e. Planned problem solving
      2. Preoperational stage (two to seven years)
         a. Symbols are used for representation
         b. Conservation is lacking
         c. Centration, or focusing on one aspect of a problem, is common
         d. Thinking is irreversible
         e. Thinking focuses on states
         f. Perceptions of the world are egocentric
      3. Concrete operational stage (seven to eleven years)
         a. Conservation abilities emerge
         b. Can arrange objects in order according to one attribute
         c. Transitivity skill is mastered
         d. Class inclusion is understood
      4. Formal operational stage (eleven years to adulthood)

        a. Can deal with hypotheticals
        b. Problem-solving is systematic
        c. Formal thought provides the basis for higher-order cognitive skills
C. Criticisms and revisions of Piaget's theory
    1. "Development precedes learning" has been challenged
    2. Possible underestimation of children's abilities
D. Theory into practice: Piaget's theory of cognitive development

II. Piaget's Theory of Cognitive Development
A. Principal concepts in Piaget's theory
    1. Schemes
    2. Assimilation
    3. Accommodation
    4. Equilibration
B. The stages
    1. Sensorimotor stage (birth to two years)
        a. Initially governed by reflexes
        b. Intentional behavior emerges next
        c. Object permanence develops
        d. Trial-and-error learning
        e. Planned problem solving
    2. Preoperational stage (two to seven years)
        a. Symbols are used for representation
        b. Conservation is lacking
        c. Centration, or focusing on one aspect of a problem, is common
        d. Thinking is irreversible
        e. Thinking focuses on states
        f. Perceptions of the world are egocentric
    3. Concrete operational stage (seven to eleven years)
        a. Conservation abilities emerge
        b. Can arrange objects in order according to one attribute
        c. Transitivity skill is mastered
        d. Class inclusion is understood
    4. Formal operational stage (eleven years to adulthood)
        a. Can deal with hypotheticals
        b. Problem-solving is systematic
        c. Formal thought provides the basis for higher-order cognitive skills
C. Criticisms and revisions of Piaget's theory
    1. "Development precedes learning" has been challenged
    2. Possible underestimation of children's abilities
D. Theory into practice: Piaget's theory of cognitive development

III. Erikson's Theory of Personal and Social Development
   A. The Stages
      1. Stage I: trust vs. mistrust (birth to eighteen months)
      2. Stage II: autonomy vs. doubt (eighteen months to three years)
      3. Stage III: initiative vs. guilt (three to six years)
      4. Stage IV: industry vs. inferiority (six to twelve years)
      5. Stage V: identity vs. role confusion (twelve to eighteen years)
      6. Stage VI: intimacy vs. isolation (young adulthood)
      7. Stage VII: generativity vs. self-absorption (middle adulthood)
      8. Stage VIII: integrity vs. despair (late adulthood)
   B. Teachers on teaching: Personal and social development
   C. Theory into practice: Personal and social development
      1. Helping students with the industry vs. inferiority crisis
      2. Helping students with the identity vs. role confusion crisis

IV. Moral Reasoning
   A. Piaget's theory of moral development
      1. Heteronomous morality
      2. Autonomous morality
   B. Kohlberg's stages of moral reasoning
      1. Preconventional
      2. Conventional
      3. Postconventional
   C. Limitations of Kohlberg's theory
   D. Teachers on teaching: Moral reasoning

V. Relationships Among Major Theories

Summary/Study Questions/Suggested Readings

CHAPTER OBJECTIVES

1. List ways in which elementary school children differ in intellectual ability from secondary school students.
2. Describe the important cognitive characteristics of children who are in the grade you would like to teach.
3. Describe the personality crises faced by (1) preschoolers and kindergartners, (2) elementary school children, and (3) high school students.
4. Describe what attitudes it is hoped children will be left with after undergoing the social and emotional crises that occur during the school years. List how teachers can help children develop a healthy, balanced outlook on life.
5. Describe how people progress in their moral reasoning abilities from simple compliance with authority to development of personal principles.

MATCHING WARM-UPS

Match the numbers of the descriptions on the right to the corresponding items on the left. A given item from the right column may be used more than once or not at all.

Quiz 1: Piaget's Theory

_____	a. Formal operations	1. Exploring with one's body
_____	b. Preoperations	2. Language develops
_____	c. Concrete operations	3. Change existing schemes
_____	d. Sensorimotor	4. Conservation develops
_____	e. Assimilation	5. Abstract reasoning
_____	f. Accommodation	6. Incorporate within existing schemes

Quiz 2: Erikson's Theory

_____	a. Industry vs. inferiority	1. Birth to 18 months
_____	b. Trust vs. mistrust	2. 18 months to 3 yrs.
_____	c. Autonomy vs. doubt	3. 3 yrs. to 6 yrs.
_____	d. Intimacy vs. isolation	4. 6 yrs. to 12 yrs.
_____	e. Identify vs. role confusion	5. 12 yrs. to 18 yrs.
_____	f. Integrity vs. despair	6. Young adulthood
_____	g. Generativity vs. self-absorption	7. Middle adulthood
_____	h. Initiative vs. guilt	8. Late adulthood

Quiz 3: Kohlberg's Theory

Note: Column B choices are each used twice.

_____	a. "Law and Order"	1. Preconventional
_____	b. Social contract	2. Conventional
_____	c. Punishment and Obedience	3. Postconventional
_____	d. Universal Ethical Principle	
_____	e. Instrumental Relativist	
_____	f. "Good boy-Good girl"	

Quiz 4: Notable Names

_____	a. Postconventional level	1. Piaget
_____	b. Psychosocial theory	2. Erikson
_____	c. Proximal Zone	3. Milne
_____	d. Moral dilemmas	4. Kohlberg
_____	e. Cognitive theory	5. Vygotsky
_____	f. Conservation	
_____	g. Initiative vs. guilt	
_____	h. Autonomous morality	

KEY TERMS

Fill in the blanks below with the letters identifying the following concepts. Each concept is used one time only.

A. Stage theories
B. Schemes
C. Assimilation
D. Accommodation
E. Equilibration
F. Sensorimotor
G. Reflexes
H. Object permanence
I. Preoperational
J. Conservation
K. Centration
L. Reversibility
M. Operations
N. Egocentric
O. Concrete operational
P. Perceived appearance
Q. Inferred reality
R. Formal operational
S. Proximal zone of development
T. Psychosocial theory
U. Unidimensional classroom
V. Multidimensional classroom
W. Heteronomous morality
X. Autonomous morality
Y. Moral dilemmas

1. Children focusing on _____ see something based on how it looks to the eye.

2. _____, as exemplified in Erikson's work, relates principles of psychological and social development.

3. The ability to perform a mental operation and then change direction in thinking is _____.

4. An uneven progression from infancy to adulthood, through a series of steps, is assumed by a(n) _____ of development.

5. During the _____ stage, children develop logical reasoning skills and can understand increasingly complex conservation problems.

6. Infants explore the world by using their senses and motor skills during the _____ stage of development.

7. Perception that is influenced by the contextual meaning of something rather than its outward appearance is called _____.

8. Understanding that stimuli which are blocked from view still exist is the notion of _____.

9. According to Piaget, the moral stage at which children believe that rules are inflexible and must be literally obeyed is _____.

10. The principle of _____ states that changing the shape of an object does not change its quantity.

11. People develop the ability to use abstract thinking during the _____ stage.

12. Hypothetical situations that require a person to judge values of right or wrong are called _____.

13. The process of restoring balance between what is understood and what is encountered is _____.

14. The mental patterns that direct behavior are called _____.

15. Preschoolers' inability to take someone else's perspective illustrates their _____ thought.

16. Reversible mental processes are called _____.

17. Focusing on only one aspect of an object, such as its height, is an example of _____.

18. Many paths to success exist in a(n) _____, whereas a single success standard is established in a(n) _____.

19. According to Piaget, the moral stage at which rules are viewed as changeable products of negotiation by people is _____.

20. Young children develop language and begin to mentally represent things during the _____ stage of development.

21. Incorporating new objects or events into existing schemes is called _____.

22. Skills that are just beyond children's capacity to assimilate lie at the _____.

23. Changing existing schemes to fit new objects is the process of _____.

24. Natural responses that do not require learning are _____.

COMPLETION QUESTIONS

1. The process of restoring mental balance when new experiences differ from present understanding is _____.

2. The belief in a smooth developmental progression is emphasized in a _____ theory of human development.

3. A child who is used to eating soup with a spoon tries to use a fork for the same purpose. The cognitive process illustrated by this behavior is _____.

4. The Piagetian stage in which conservation abilities emerge and develop is _____.

5. The Piagetian stage in which most adolescents function is _____.

6. During the _____ stage, learning depends mostly on physical interactions with the environment.

7. The process of changing an existing scheme in response to new experiences is _____.

8. Children who have acquired _____ will search for a toy that is not presently visible.

9. After having identified two balls of clay as being equal in quantity, a child watches one ball being rolled into a sausage shape. He then indicates that it (the sausage) is larger than the ball-shaped piece. This child apparently lacks the principle of _____.

10. Being able to perform a mental operation and then return to the starting point represents _____ thinking.

11. A preoperational child responds to _____ appearances of stimuli, whereas the older, concrete operational child responds to _____ reality.

12. A child who is almost, but not quite ready to master conservation is at the _____ of development for that skill.

13. Psychosocial theory, the focus of Erikson's work, relates principles of _____ and _____ development.

14. According to Erikson, the main psychosocial crisis that faces the young adult is _____.

15. The significant figure is the child's mother during the _____ stage of Erikson's scheme.

16. The main psychosocial conflict for adolescents is identity vs. _____.

17. A frequent source of conflict during the _____ psychosocial stage is often toilet training.

18. _____ classrooms are those in which children are shown many alternate paths to success.

19. Piaget's label for the first stage of morality in which children see rules as inflexible is _____ morality.

20. The most sophisticated moral reasoning level in Kohlberg's scheme occurs during the _____ stage.

MULTIPLE-CHOICE

Select the best answer for each of the following items.

1. Which of the following best illustrates Piaget's notion of equilibration?

   a. Turning on the TV and watching a favorite show
   b. Trying to memorize the Pledge of Allegiance
   c. Trying to reconcile how the local police chief could be convicted of a crime
   d. Reading in the paper that the star high school basketball player scored 32 points last night

2. Which of the following shows a correct matching between Piagetian stage and its approximate age range?

   a. Formal operational : 7 to 11
   b. Preoperational : 7 to 11
   c. Sensorimotor : 2 to 7
   d. Preoperational : 2 to 7

3. Which of the following sayings best conveys the meaning of object permanence?

   a. "A penny saved is a penny earned."
   b. "Whatever goes up must come down."
   c. "Damn the torpedoes, full speed ahead."
   d. "Out of sight, out of mind."

4. Mastery of conservation skills is acquired during the _____ stage.

   a. preoperational
   b. sensorimotor
   c. formal operational
   d. concrete operational

5. A child is shown two identical rows of 10 pennies each. After identifying the two rows as equal, he watches the examiner spread the 10 pennies apart in one row, making that row longer. The child now confidently proclaims that the latter row contains more pennies. One can infer that this child is operating in the _____ stage.

   a. preoperational
   b. sensorimotor
   c. formal operational
   d. concrete operational

6. Which of the following illustrates a reversible operation?

   a. 6 + 5 = 11, then 6 + 6 = 12
   b. 5 x 8 = 40, then 8 x 5 = 40
   c. 4 - 1 = 3, then 3 + 1 = 4
   d. 2 x 2 = 4, then 4 - 2 = 2

7. Children standing on the roof of a very tall building gaze down at a red moving van stopped at a light. Which of the following responses would most clearly reflect reliance on perceived appearance?

   a. "The truck is probably fast."
   b. "Look at that tiny truck."
   c. "The truck can probably hold a lot of furniture."
   d. "I wonder who's moving."

8. Which of the following processes is a major contributor to children's inability to solve conservation problems?

   a. Centration
   b. Equilibration
   c. Combination
   d. Object permanence

9. Which of the following abilities is characteristic of the formal operations stage?

   a. Abstract thinking
   b. Systematic problem solving
   c. Adult-like thinking
   d. All of the above

10. A major criticism of Piaget's theory concerns his

   a. use of behavioristic methods in studying humans.
   b. possible underestimation of children's abilities.
   c. assumption that learning precedes development.
   d. emphasis on the importance of accelerating children's progression through stages.

11. An implication of Piaget's theory for elementary school teaching is to

   a. introduce abstract thinking early in the curriculum.
   b. provide a substantial amount of direct (teacher-centered) instruction.
   c. increase use of discovery learning exercises.
   d. keep the instructional level just below children's proximal level of development.

12. Erikson's theory can be described as a _____ theory.

a. stage
b. discontinuous
c. psychosocial
d. all of the above

13. Which of the following represents a correct sequence of stages?

a. Trust vs. mistrust, then autonomy vs. doubt
b. Initiative vs. guilt, then autonomy vs. doubt
c. Integrity vs. despair, then generativity vs. self-absorption
d. Identity vs. role confusion, then industry vs. inferiority

14. Peer groups become a central influence during Erikson's _____ stage.

a. intimacy vs. isolation
b. integrity vs. despair
c. trust vs. mistrust
d. identity vs. role confusion

15. Which of the following Eriksonian stages overlaps to some degree with Piaget's preoperations stage?

a. Autonomy vs. doubt
b. Industry vs. inferiority
c. Initiative vs. guilt
d. All of the above

16. Which of the following teaching practices do researchers such as Entwistle and Hayduk view as potentially harmful to successful resolution of the industry vs. inferiority crisis?

a. Criterion-referenced grading
b. Oral recitations
c. Ability grouping
d. Frequent testing

17. Multidimensional classrooms are specifically intended to

a. use different teachers and sections of the room for different subjects.
b. build self-concept by providing alternate ways to succeed.
c. select the top students and top groups from a class.
d. incorporate the values and languages of multicultural groups.

18. A student is caught breaking a class rule. A child in Piaget's heteronomous stage of morality is likely to react in support of

   a. viewing punishment as deserved regardless of the circumstances.
   b. discussing the offense and taking a class vote on whether a punishment is in order.
   c. giving the offender the opportunity to defend his behavior.
   d. trying to protect the offender by covering up for him.

19. In which of Kohlberg's stages are the laws of society seen as somewhat arbitrary and thus flexible under certain circumstances?

   a. Postconventional
   b. Conventional
   c. Preconventional
   d. Unconventional

20. Erikson's theory differs somewhat from those of Piaget and Kohlberg by

   a. incorporating children and adolescents only.
   b. seeing the movement through stages as relatively automatic rather than a function of disequilibrium.
   c. allowing for backward as well as forward movement.
   d. recognizing but deemphasizing the influences of other people in the developmental process.

<u>APPLICATION:</u> Conservation

Explore Piaget's conservation principles by administering the following task to individuals of ages 5-6, 8-10, and over 13:

Present the subject with two equal-sized balls of clay. Allow him or her to hold the clay balls. Then ask whether one ball has more clay or whether they both have the same amount. Then roll one of the balls into a sausage shape, allow the subject to hold the two pieces, and ask the same question. Then roll the sausage-shaped clay back into a ball and ask the question for a third time.

A. Based on Piagetian theory, what would be expected responses to the three questions?
B. What were the actual responses of <u>your</u> subjects?
C. Based on your experiences as "examiner" do you feel that it is possible to <u>teach</u> conservation skills to nonconservers? Explain.

<u>APPLICATION:</u> Piagetian Stages

Based on the brief descriptions provided below, try to classify the individuals concerned in terms of the four Piagetian stages (see answer section to check your selection).

A. This individual is approximately two years old, and is verbally advanced. She identifies and names different objects, asks her parents to take her places, to give her things, etc.

B. This individual is a second-grader. When talking to other children he doesn't listen to or process much of what is being said, but focuses instead on <u>his</u> own commentary. Since he likes art in school and dislikes gym class, he assumes that others feel the exact same way. He is quite demanding at home, because he assumes that his parents are "there" to serve him.

C. This individual is approximately two years old, but not very proficient verbally. He likes building towers out of blocks and is very creative at it. If a piece doesn't fit as he wants, he studies the pattern and tries a new strategy. But, if asked to verbalize the solution, he is unable to do so.

D. This individual is in the eighth grade. She plays a game on a computer that asks her to guess a number between 1 and 100. She tries 99, but the computer responds "TOO HIGH." She then tries 10 and the computer responds "TOO LOW." She tries 20 next ("TOO LOW"), then 25 ("TOO LOW"), then 30 ("TOO LOW"). Six tries later she identifies the correct number, 52.

E. This individual is in the seventh grade. He is also playing the number game just described (in "D"). His first guess is 50 ("TOO HIGH"), so next he tries 25, reasoning that if incorrect, he can eliminate half the remaining values. The computer responds ("TOO HIGH"), so he tries 12 next ("TOO LOW"), using the same reasoning. Two trials later he guesses the correct number, 21.

<u>APPLICATION:</u> Psychosocial Stages

Identify the psychosocial stage (from Erikson) most clearly represented by each of the following situations.

A. The individual desperately wants to be given a bid to a sorority, and feels that her life "may be over" if that need is denied.

B. The individual looks over his life accomplishments and wonders what, if anything, there is to strive for next. "Have I done anything useful?", he questions.

C. This person's main interest is with school accomplishments and gaining approval from the teacher. She walks out of the class beaming after receiving an "A" on her math test. She is now thinking of herself as "someone who is good in math."

D. This individual wants to demonstrate her independence and skill at performing things. She hopes that her mother will let her ride her bike in the street so that she can extend the distance and speed achieved the day before.

E. This individual is growing tired of "hanging out" with his friends and being alone at other times. He senses a need to settle down and obtain more stability in his life. He even begins considering "popping the question" to Jo Ann, his steady girl friend.

COMPUTER EXERCISE: Moral Development

The EDUCATIONAL PSYCHOLOGY COMPUTER DISK for your text contains a program called "Moral Development." The exercise presents a series of brief stories or "vignettes" each describing a behavior by an individual. Following the vignette is an evaluation by another person regarding the appropriateness of that behavior. Your task is to consider that second person's evaluation and classify him/her into one of Kohlberg's three major stages on that basis (i.e., as preconventional, conventional, or postconventional). Here is a sample situation:

Vignette: Jules, whose family is economically disadvantaged, had little dinner last night and no breakfast this morning. During the morning recess he steals an apple from Emily's lunch box and eats it. He is caught by the teacher in the next room.

Observer's Evaluation: Jules is definitely wrong because he got caught. Now the teacher will punish him for sure. He should know that teachers are constantly on the look out for that sort of thing.

Your Response: Based on the above evaluation, into which moral stage would you classify the observer?

a. Preconventional
b. Conventional
c. Postconventional

Answer: Preconventional would be correct. The observer appears to be basing his/her "morality" decision on whether one gets caught rather than on the nature of the behavior relative to existing local or societal rules.

The computer program contains many more of these, with interactive feedback! See how many you can answer correctly on the first try.

COMPUTER EXERCISE: Conservation Tasks

The EDUCATIONAL PSYCHOLOGY COMPUTER DISK for your text contains two simulation programs, one labeled VOLUME and the other BEAKERS. Each takes you through the steps of a Piagetian conservation task. VOLUME establishes the computer as the interviewer and the user as the subject (or child). Based on the latter's responses, it then classifies him/her into one of the Piagetian stages. BEAKERS tests the way in which the subject solves a logical problem and evaluates whether the strategy is indicative of formal operations reasoning. More information on the procedures and background for both programs is provided in the USER'S

GUIDE for the disk. (Also see the Chapter 3 Applications section in this book for more information on BEAKERS.

ESSAY/DISCUSSION

1. Differentiate between a continuous theory and a stage theory. Use one of the theories in Chapter 2 to illustrate the latter.

2. Identify Piaget's four stages and discuss each with regard to implications for child care or teaching.

3. For each of the following age groups, characterize the cognitive, psychosocial, and moral development levels teachers are likely to encounter in their students: a) first-graders (age 6-7), b) fifth-graders (age 10-11), c) high school juniors and seniors (16-18).

4. Describe the data collection approach used by Kohlberg for studying moral development levels. Describe and defend your views regarding its validity (accuracy) for (a) describing moral development and (b) predicting moral behaviors of individuals.

5. Piaget has referred to the issue of accelerating children's progression through cognitive stages as the "American question" since it is raised so frequently by American researchers and educators. Describe your position on this issue. Do you feel that the rate of development is fixed developmentally or can it be altered through special training? More specifically, can a first-grader be taught algebra?

ANSWERS

Matching Warm-ups

Quiz 1	Quiz 2	Quiz 3	Quiz 4
a. 5 (28)	a. 4 (36)	a. 2 (43)	a. 4 (43)
b. 2 (22)	b. 1 (34)	b. 2 (43)	b. 2 (33)
c. 4 (26)	c. 2 (34)	c. 1 (43)	c. 5 (32)
d. 1 (21)	d. 6 (36)	d. 3 (43)	d. 4 (42)
e. 6 (19)	e. 5 (35)	e. 3 (43)	e. 1 (18-19)
f. 3 (20)	f. 8 (37)	f. 1 (43)	f. 1 (22)
	g. 7 (37)		g. 2 (34)
	h. 3 (34)		h. 1 (41-42)

Key Terms

1.	P (26)	9.	W (42)	17.	K (24)
2.	T (33)	10.	J (22)	18.	V;U (39)
3.	L (24)	11.	R (28)	19.	X (42)
4.	A (18)	12.	Y (42)	20.	I (22)
5.	O (26)	13.	E (20)	21.	C (19)
6.	F (21)	14.	B (19)	22.	S (32)
7.	Q (26)	15.	N (25)	23.	D (20)
8.	H (21)	16.	M (24)	24.	G (21)

Completion Questions

1. equilibration (20)
2. continuous (18)
3. assimilation (19)
4. concrete operations (26)
5. formal operations (28)
6. sensorimotor (21)
7. accommodation (20)
8. object permanence (21)
9. conservation (22)
10. reversible (24)
11. perceived; inferred (26)
12. proximal zone (32)
13. psychological; social (33)
14. intimacy vs. isolation (36)
15. trust vs. mistrust (34)
16. role confusion (35)
17. autonomy vs. doubt (34)
18. multidimensional (39)
19. heteronomous (42)
20. postconventional (43,45)

Multiple-Choice

1.	c (20)	6.	c (24)	11.	c (31)	16.	c (38)
2.	d (22)	7.	b (26)	12.	d (33)	17.	b (39)
3.	d (21)	8.	a (24)	13.	a (34-37)	18.	a (42)
4.	d (26)	9.	d (28-29)	14.	d (35)	19.	a (45)
5.	a (24)	10.	b (30)	15.	d (37)	20.	b (46)

Application: Piagetian Stages

A. Preoperations stage (language is advanced; can "think" well verbally)

B. Preoperations stage (approximately seven years of age; probably about to enter concrete operations, but appears very egocentric and inner-directed in his thought).

C. Sensorimotor (likes to work with objects; beginning to problem solve but hasn't developed proficiency in verbal reasoning).

D. Concrete operations (about 13 years old, and seems to follow feedback correctly, but does not use a very logical problem-solving strategy; compare strategy in "E").

E. Formal operations (very logical and efficient reasoning is used to solve the problem).

Application: Psychosocial Stages

A. Identity vs. role confusion
B. Integrity vs. despair
C. Industry vs. inferiority
D. Initiative vs. guilt
E. Intimacy vs. isolation

3 Development During Childhood and Adolescence

CHAPTER OUTLINE

I. Development During Early Childhood
   A. Physical development
      1. Fine motor activities
      2. Gross motor activities
      3. Implications of physical development for preschool education
   B. Cognitive abilities
      1. The preoperational child
   C. Language
      1. Verbal language
      2. Transformational grammar
      3. Reading
      4. Writing
   D. Early childhood education
      1. Day-care programs
      2. Nursery schools
      3. Compensatory preschool programs
      4. Kindergarten programs
      5. The preschool years: A critical period in intellectual development?
   E. Socioemotional development
      1. Psychosocial development
      2. Parenting
      3. Peer relationships
      4. Friendships
      5. Prosocial behaviors

F. Play
   1. The contributions of play to early childhood
   2. The disappearance of childhood
G. Encouraging socioemotional development
   1. Providing a variety of materials
   2. Using group games to teach cooperation
H. Theory into practice: Teaching preschoolers and kindergartners

II. Development During Middle Childhood
   A. Physical development
      1. Lower elementary children
      2. Upper elementary children
   B. Cognitive abilities
      1. Movement from egocentric thought to decentered thought
      2. Emergence of logical and reversible thinking
   C. Teachers on teaching: Elementary school teaching
   D. Socioemotional development
      1. Self-concept
      2. Emotional development
   E. Theory into practice: Teaching elementary age children

III. Development During Adolescence
   A. Physical development
      1. Variability in onset and rate of puberty
      2. Reactions to puberty
      3. Early and late maturity
   B. Cognitive abilities
      1. Piagetian theory
      2. Combinational systems
      3. Hypothetical conditions
   C. Teachers on teaching: Teaching junior high and high school students
   D. Socioemotional development
      1. Identity
      2. Autonomy
      3. Conformity
      4. Interpersonal development
      5. Intimacy
      6. Peer relations
      7. Dating
   E. Problems of adolescence
      1. Delinquency
      2. Emotional disorders
      3. Drug and alcohol abuse
      4. Pregnancy

F. Theory into practice: Teaching junior high and high school students
   1. Encouraging cognitive development
   2. Encouraging socioemotional development
   3. Personal and social development

Summary/Study Questions/Suggested Readings

CHAPTER OBJECTIVES

1. Describe how children learn about language.
2. Understand the debate over whether early childhood education should stress intellectual or social development.
3. Understand the emotional turmoil that can accompany puberty.
4. List factors that contribute to a child's identity.
5. Describe how adolescents learn to share their feelings and thoughts with friends of their own sex and with members of the opposite sex.

Matching Warm-Ups

Match the numbers of the descriptions on the right to the corresponding items on the left. A given item from the right column may be used more than once or not al all.

Quiz 1: Parenting Styles

_____ a.	Authoritarian	1. Firm but warm
_____ b.	Permissive	2. Few expectations or restrictions
_____ c.	Authoritative	3. Strict enforcement of rules

Quiz 2: Types of Play

_____ a.	Pretend	1. Acting at prescribed roles, such as in playing doctor
_____ b.	Sociodramatic	2. Coordinated activities in a group
_____ c.	Parallel	3. Imagining oneself in a make believe role
_____ d.	Cooperative	4. Playing by oneself

Quiz 3: Socioemotional Development

_____ a.	Self-concept	1. Uncertainty about one's role
_____ b.	Identity diffusion	2. Needs for intimacy and sexual gratification
_____ c.	Identity foreclosure	3. Rejection of others
_____ d.	Interpersonal theory of psychiatry	4. Early acceptance of a role to relieve uncertainty
		5. An individual's sense of who he/she is

Quiz 4: Notable Names

_____	a. Identify foreclosure	1.	J. Piaget
_____	b. Transformational grammar	2.	H. Sullivan
_____	c. Combinational systems	3.	N. Chomsky
_____	d. Parenting styles	4.	S. Freud
_____	e. Interpersonal theory of psychiatry	5.	D. Baumrind
_____	f. Classification	6.	L. Kohlberg
		7.	E. Erikson

KEY TERMS

Fill in the blanks below with the letters identifying the following concepts. Each concept is used one time only.

A. Fine motor activities
B. Gross motor activities
C. Transformational grammar
D. Readiness
E. Compensatory preschool programs
F. Parenting styles
G. Authoritarian parents
H. Permissive parents
I. Authoritative parents
J. Peers
K. Prosocial behaviors
L. Pretend Play
M. Sociodramatic play
N. Self-concept
O. Puberty
P. Reflectivity
Q. Identity diffusion
R. Identity foreclosure
S. Interpersonal theory of psychiatry

1. Parents who are warm yet demanding in interacting with their child are _____.

2. The capability of reproduction emerges during the stage of _____.

3. Chomsky's theory of _____ emphasizes the underlying ideas of verbal communication as opposed to the specific sentence structure used.

4. Choosing a role prematurely to help establish a self-concept is called _____ by Erikson.

5. Perceptions of our strengths and limitations help to form a(n) _____.

6. General patterns of behavior used at home to interact with children are _____.

7. When children transform themselves into imaginary roles or situations, they are engaged in _____.

8. Parents who require strict obedience are _____.

9. Parents who give their child considerable freedom are _____.

10. Not having a sense of one's identity is called _____ by Erikson.

11. Actions, such as running or throwing, that involve the limbs and large muscles are called _____.

12. Acting out prescribed roles, such as a "mother" or "teacher," represents _____.

13. Adolescents' interpersonal relationships and needs for security are emphasized in the _____.

14. Children who are properly prepared to perform an activity are said to have _____ for that task.

15. Actions that show concern and respect for others are _____.

16. Movements requiring precision and dexterity are called _____.

17. The tendency to think about one's own thoughts is called _____.

18. Advance preparation for disadvantaged children to help them succeed in lower elementary school grades is provided by _____.

19. Children who are equal in status to one another are called _____.

COMPLETION QUESTIONS

1. Children who play by themselves in the proximity of others are engaged in _____ play.

2. _____ theory emphasizes the equivalence of languages and dialects that can express the same ideas.

3. _____ programs primarily exist to provide child-care services, whereas _____ programs are designed to promote readiness for entering school.

4. Head Start, which was initiated during the Johnson administration, is an example of a _____ program.

5. According to Erikson's theory, preschool children must resolve the personality crisis of _____.

6. Research on parenting styles suggests that _____ parents tend to raise more productive and better adjusted children than do other types of parents.

7. Other than parents, the most important influence on children's development are their _____ or equals.

8. Actions that show respect and caring for others are called ____ behaviors.

9. Physical actions such as drawing or tying a shoe comprise _____ activities.

10. Girls are slightly shorter and lighter than boys until about the age of _____, when the two sexes are equal in size.

11. At age 12, the majority of children are in the _____ stage of development in Piaget's scheme.

12. The three major influences on a child's social development during primary grades are _____, _____, and _____.

13. A person's feelings about his/her strengths and weaknesses help to form his/her _____.

14. An individual becomes sexually mature at the time of _____.

15. During adolescence the development of _____ operations begins to emerge in most adolescents, allowing them to interpret abstract relationships much more easily.

16. Adolescents who begin to study themselves and think about their own thoughts are demonstrating the process of _____.

17. Identity _____ is when adolescents adopt a role prematurely to escape the problems of identity _____, the absence of clear identity.

18. Adolescents strive for increased _____, the freedom to self-determine actions and choices.

19. Sullivan's interpersonal theory of psychiatry is oriented primarily around the adolescent's need for _____ from other people.

MULTIPLE-CHOICE

Select the best answer for each of the following items.

1. One child says "I am about to depart for the cinema." Another says "I'm splitting for the videos." Transformation grammar theory would emphasize the

   a. more sophisticated language used by the first child.
   b. better syntax used by the first child.
   c. likelihood of the first child being a better reasoner than the second child.
   d. similarity between the underlying ideas of the two expressions.

2. Language begins to develop

a. about age 2-3.
b. about age 3-4.
c. about the time children enter school.
d. during the late preoperations stage.

3. An example of a gross motor activity is

a. climbing a tree.
b. drawing a man.
c. peeling a potato.
d. all of these.

4. Day-care programs exist primarily to

a. teach readiness skills for entering school.
b. teach remedial skills to disadvantaged children.
c. provide child-care services for working parents.
d. a. and c.

5. During the past few years the function of kindergarten has shifted increasingly toward

a. social skills development.
b. day-care functions.
c. physical education and health.
d. academic training.

6. Research on early childhood education programs appears to indicate that preschool programs

a. are crucial for all children.
b. have little short-term effect but strong positive effects over time.
c. have little influence on learning.
d. are more critical for lower-class than for middle-class children.

7. According to Erik Erikson's theory, during early childhood (in the preschool years), the child must resolve the personality crisis of

a. autonomy vs. doubt.
b. intimacy vs. isolation.
c. initiative vs. guilt.
d. identity vs. identity diffusion.

8. Which of the following statements about parenting styles is true?

   a. Authoritarian parents demand obedience which they enforce mainly through verbal interchanges.
   b. Authoritative parents tend to give their children as much freedom as possible.
   c. Authoritative parents tend to have children who lack self-esteem and achievement motivation.
   d. Authoritative parents are both warm and demanding in interactions with their children.

9. According to many developmentalists such as Elkind, the period of childhood in today's society is

   a. being lengthened by overprotective parents.
   b. much the same as it was 100 years ago.
   c. disappearing as children are pressured more and more to achieve.
   d. poorly understood by psychologists.

10. Which of the following is thought to promote prosocial behaviors?

   a. Warm, responsive parent-child relationships
   b. Contact with caring adults
   c. Exposure to nonaggressive solutions
   d. All of the above

11. What type of play develops earliest?

   a. Sociodramatic
   b. Cooperative
   c. Parallel
   d. None of the above; all develop about the same time

12. Physical growth during the early elementary school years is

   a. much more rapid for girls than for boys.
   b. slower than in early childhood.
   c. much more rapid for boys than for girls.
   d. greater for muscular development than for skeletal development.

13. Which of the following statements about physical growth of upper elementary children is true?

   a. Resistance to fatigue and disease decreases.
   b. Boys begin their growth spurt a year earlier than girls.
   c. Both girls and boys experience a growth spurt after puberty is reached.
   d. Ten- and eleven-year-olds may become less coordinated than when they were younger.

14. Which of the following is <u>not</u> one of the Piagetian tasks that concrete operational children can typically perform?

   a. Number
   b. Classification
   c. Conservation
   d. Hypothetical conditions

15. During the primary grades, the <u>major</u> influence that shapes children's social development is

   a. the school experience.
   b. parents and family.
   c. the peer group.
   d. television.

16. Which of the following is <u>not</u> recommended as a teaching strategy for elementary school children?

   a. Rules should be set by teachers only, without modification based on children's views.
   b. Make instruction concrete and experiential.
   c. Avoid labeling students according to their performances.
   d. Use an authoritative teaching style.

17. According to Peskin's research, early maturers

   a. develop a more positive self-concept during puberty.
   b. need more help than late maturers in school work.
   c. experience a relatively difficult adjustment later in high school.
   d. have a relatively difficult adjustment at the time of puberty.

18. Select the descriptor that does <u>not</u> apply to typical adolescent cognitive abilities.

   a. Abstract reasoning
   b. Can deal with hypotheticals
   c. Irreversible thinking
   d. Combinational solutions

19. Which of the following predictions about adolescents is consistent with the Interpersonal Theory of Psychiatry?

a. They have a strong need for sexual contact but little for intimacy.
b. Their needs for intimacy are usually greater than those for sexual gratification.
c. Relative to their childhood years, their needs for significant relationships are lower.
d. Attempts at intimate communication usually first occur with opposite-sex friends.

20. Which of the following descriptions of adolescent experiences most clearly illustrates <u>identity foreclosure?</u>

a. Since John is confused about his identity, he decides to take some time to experiment with different roles.
b. Since Maria is a good science student, loves helping others, and has parents who are both doctors, she is considering pursuing a career in medicine.
c. Warren, who is troubled and confused about "his direction" in life, decides that he will become a lawyer, since lawyers seem confident and capable.
d. Raoul alternately decides that he will become a professional baseball player, a psychologist, a banker, or maybe just stay in the neighborhood for awhile.

<u>APPLICATION:</u> Teaching Elementary Children

Read each of the following descriptions and indicate (a) what you feel the student's problems and needs are and (b) what teaching/intervention strategies you might use to help the individual.

A. Marcia is a sad-faced usually listless fifth-grader. Her most distinguishing (or obvious) characteristic is being over-weight, which is certainly a contributing factor to her low energy, poor performance in gym classes, and low popularity. Despite being an above average achiever in all subjects and exceptional in art, Marcia is rarely sought out by others or invited to participate in group social activities. In team competitions such as spelling bees, Marcia is usually picked close to last. Your feeling is that Marcia has excellent academic potential that, along with her social development, is being hampered by these problems.

B. Julius, a sixth-grader, is clearly the best athlete and one of the most popular students in the class. While most of the other boys still look like children, Julius has the appearance and voice of a young man, tall and muscular with facial hair that forms a shadow of a beard and moustache. These physical characteristics give him even more self-confidence and greater advantages over his peers in sports such as football and basketball. The problem is that although Julius is close to average in academic ability, he has completely abandoned his schoolwork. He is failing every subject (except physical education). In class he rarely listens or takes notes, but intermittently looks out the window, stares into space, or doodles in his notebook. As soon as class ends, he's out in the hall in a flash where he can assume his position as "heart throb" to the female students and "athletic hero" to the males.

APPLICATION: Identifying Developmental Events

Classify each of the following events as typically associated with:

a. early childhood (2-6)
b. middle childhood (7-prepuberty)
c. adolescence (at puberty)

1. Concrete operations is reached
2. Initiative vs. guilt stage
3. Sexual maturity is reached
4. Delinquency may be a problem
5. Friends are momentary relationships
6. Sociodramatic play
7. Preoperational stage
8. Formal operations is established
9. Conservation and classification abilities are acquired
10. Decentered thinking begins

APPLICATION: Field Study

The purpose of this exercise is to apply developmental concepts to an individual observed in a real-life setting. To accomplish this purpose, visit a class or field setting and:

1. Select one student as the target individual for your developmental observations and reporting.

2. Each time you visit the class or field setting be sure to pay special attention to your target individual.

3. Use the developmental areas listed below as a guide to observing and taking notes on your target individual's development.

4. Use the observational information obtained for completing the written report below.
   A. Physical Development

      1. Describe the target individual's physical appearance (i.e. height, weight, and dress), gross and fine motor skills.

      2. Was the target individual above, within, or below his/her age group norms of physical development?

Age: _____ yrs. old   Gross motor: _____
Height: _____   Fine motor: _____
Weight: _____

B. Cognitive Development

1. Describe the behaviors that indicate the individual's cognitive skills.

2. Do you feel that the target individual is above, within, or below his/her age group norms of cognitive development? Describe why.

3. Piagetian Stage: ______________________________
Name Stage
What characteristics of this stage were observed?

4. Describe the individual's:
Language ability ______________________________
Intellectual ability ______________________________

C. Social-Emotional Development

1. Describe the behavioral indicators of social, peer, and emotional development observed.

2. Was the target individual's social behaviors typical for his/her age? Describe how.

3. Do you think the target individual is popular and an "in-group" member? Describe why.

4. Do you think the target individual is successfully resolving his/her Eriksonian psychosocial development crisis? Describe why and indicate the Eriksonian stage involved.

COMPUTER EXERCISE: Combinational Thinking

The EDUCATIONAL PSYCHOLOGY COMPUTER DISK for your text contains a program called "Beakers." It provides a test of combinational thinking similar to the task described in your textbook. Specifically, it presents four beakers of clear liquids and asks you to try to determine which individual liquid or combination of liquids produces a particular result. Since the program randomly selects a different correct combination for each new task, it can be used by the same person more than once to try out different response strategies. A special feature of the program is its analysis of the logic of the strategy used, and identification of unsystematic problem-solving responses. Some suggestions.

1. Try the program yourself to test your own performance.

2. See if you can understand the two systematic strategies that it monitors (these are called "Strategies 1 & 2" on the disk and in the User's Guide).

3. Test several children at different ages. What strategies do younger (age 8 or 9) subjects use? Older subjects (over 12)?

4. Would adminstering the task by computer rather than with real objects make it more or less difficult in your opinion? Explain.

ESSAY/DISCUSSION

1. What influences can parenting have on children's development? Discuss your views on this issue while contrasting Baumrind's three parenting styles with regard to their orientation and effectiveness.

2. In recent years certain nursery school programs have increased emphasis on teaching basic skills while limiting opportunities for free play. Describe and support your reactions to this orientation.

3. Characterize development patterns of physical growth from early childhood through adolescence. Identify differences that occur for females and males.

4. Adolescence has been described by psychologists as a time of "storm and stress." Discuss adolescence from this perspective, indicating the major types of pressures experienced during the adolescent years.

5. Good teachers recognize the importance of adapting instructional and interpersonal strategies to students' development levels. Describe the cognitive and social characteristics of students in the following three stages, and indicate what types of teaching strategies, in your opinion, would work best at each stage. Stages: Early childhood, middle childhood, and adolescence.

ANSWERS

Matching Warm-Ups

Quiz 1	Quiz 2	Quiz 3	Quiz 4
a. 3 (58)	a. 3 (60)	a. 5 (69)	a. 7 (80)
b. 2 (58)	b. 1 (60)	b. 1 (80)	b. 3 (54)
c. 1 (58)	c. 4 (60)	c. 4 (80)	c. 1 (76)
	d. 2 (60)	d. 2 (82)	d. 5 (58)
			e. 2 (82)
			f. 1 (66)

Key Terms

1.	I (58)	11.	B (52)
2.	O (74)	12.	M (60)
3.	C (54)	13.	S (82)
4.	R (80)	14.	D (56)
5.	N (69)	15.	K (59)
6.	F (58)	16.	A (52)
7.	L (60)	17.	P (79)
8.	G (58)	18.	E (56)
9.	H (58)	19.	J (59)
10.	Q (80)		

Completion Questions

1. parallel (60)
2. transformational grammar (54)
3. day care; nursery school (55-56)
4. compensatory preschool (56)
5. initiative vs. guilt (58)
6. authoritative (58)
7. peers (59)
8. prosocial (59)
9. fine motor (52)
10. nine (64)
11. concrete operations (65-66)
12. parents; peers; school experiences (70)
13. self-concept (69)
14. puberty (74)
15. formal (76)
16. reflectivity (79)
17. foreclosure; diffusion (80)
18. autonomy (81)
19. intimacy (82)

Multiple-Choice

1.	d (54)	6.	d (57)	11.	c (60)	16.	a (73-74)
2.	a (53)	7.	c (58)	12.	b (64)	17.	d (75)
3.	a (52)	8.	d (58)	13.	d (65)	18.	c (76-77)
4.	c (55)	9.	c (61)	14.	d (66)	19.	b (82)
5.	d (57)	10.	d (59)	15.	b (70)	20.	c (80)

Application: Identifying Developmental Events

1.	b (65-66)	6.	a (60)
2.	a (58)	7.	a (52-53)
3.	c (74)	8.	c (76)
4.	c (84)	9.	b (66)
5.	a (59)	10.	b (67)

4 Behavioral Theories of Learning

CHAPTER OUTLINE

I. What is Learning?
   A. Experience as the key factor
   b. How learning takes place

II. Theories of Learning

III. Evolution of Behavioral Learning Theories
   A. Ivan Pavlov: Classical conditioning
      1. Pavlov's experiment
      2. Classical conditioning components
   B. E.L. Thorndike: The Law of Effect
      1. S-R Theory
      2. Law of Effect
   C. B.F. Skinner: Operant Conditioning
      1. The nature of operant behaviors
      2. Apparatus and procedures for Skinner's research

IV. Principles of Behavioral Learning Theories
   A. Consequences
      1. Effects of consequences in strenghtening and weakening behaviors
      2. Reinforcers and punishers

   B. Reinforcers
      1. Definition of reinforcer
      2. Types of reinforcers
      3. Positive and negative reinforcers
      4. Premack Principle

5. Teachers on teaching: Strategies for reinforcement
6. Theory into practice: Classroom uses of reinforcement

C. Punishers
   1. Punishment I
   2. Punishment II
D. Immediacy of consequences
   1. Effectiveness of immediate vs. delayed feedback
   2. Purposes of immediate feedback
   3. Practical limitations in classroom uses
E. Shaping
   1. What shaping is
   2. Using chaining to break tasks into small steps
   3. Reverse chaining
   4. Teachers on teaching: Encouraging desirable behavior
F. Extinction
   1. The effects of withdrawing reinforcers
   2. Applications of extinction in modifying behavior
   3. Decreasing extinction time by informing individual that reinforcement will not occur
G. Schedules of reinforcement
   1. Fixed ratio
   2. Variable ratio
   3. Fixed interval
   4. Variable interval
   5. Teachers on teaching: Reinforcement schedules
   6. Influences of different schedules on extinction rate
H. Maintenance
I. Antecedent stimuli
   1. The function of antecedent stimuli as cues for what will be reinforced or punished
   2. Stimulus discrimination
J. Discrimination
   1. Discriminative stimuli
   2. Classroom uses of discriminative stimuli
K. Generalization
   1. Examples of generalization
   2. Dependency of generalization on similarity of settings

V. Social Learning Theory

A. Modeling
   1. Attentional phase
   2. Retention phase
   3. Reproduction phase
   4. Motivational phase
   5. Vicarious learning
   6. Teachers on teaching: Modeling

B. Self-Regulation
   1. Rationale for self-regulation strategies
   2. Research on self-regulation training

VI. Applications of Behavioral Learning Theories

VII. Strengths and Limitations of Behavioral Theories of Learning
   A. A restricted focus on observable behavior
   B. Relationship to cognitive models

Summary/Study Questions/Suggested Readings

LEARNING OBJECTIVES

1. Define learning.
2. Describe experiments that led to the theories of classical and operant conditioning, and describe differences between these theories.
3. Define reinforcement and give classroom examples of positive and negative reinforcement.
4. Explain the difference between negative reinforcement and punishment, and describe how these are used in schools.
5. Describe how teachers can use shaping to help students learn complex skills.
6. List the four types of reinforcement schedules.
7. Define observational learning, or modeling, and give examples of things you have learned this way.

MATCHING WARM-UPS

Match the numbers of the descriptions on the right to the corresponding items on the left. A given item from the right column may be used more than once or not at all.

Quiz 1: Classical Conditioning (Pavlov's Experiment)

_____ a. Unconditioned stimulus		1. Bell
_____ b. Unconditioned response		2. Salivating to bell
_____ c. Neutral stimulus		3. Salivating to meat
_____ d. Conditioned response		4. Meat

Quiz 2: Types of Reinforcers

_____ a. Positive reinforcement	1. Administer aversive stimulus
_____ b. Negative reinforcement	2. Remove reinforcer
_____ c. Punishment I	3. Remove aversive stimulus
_____ d. Punishment II	4. Administer reinforcer

Quiz 3: Schedules of Reinforcement

_____ a.	Fixed interval	1.	Reward after constant time period
_____ b.	Variable interval	2.	Reward after constant number of responses
_____ c.	Fixed ratio	3.	Reward after every response
_____ d.	Variable ratio	4.	Reward after unpredictable time period
		5.	Reward after unpredictable number of responses

Quiz 4: Notable Names

_____ a.	Operant conditioning	1.	Thorndike
_____ b.	Social learning theory	2.	Pavlov
_____ c.	Skinner Box (a rough one, be careful!)	3.	Bandura
_____ d.	Law of Effect	4.	Skinner
_____ e.	Four-phase model of observational learning		
_____ f.	Used dogs in his classic experiment		
_____ g.	Exclusively used people in research		
_____ h.	Primarily used rats and pigeons in research		
_____ i.	Used cats and puzzle boxes in classic research		

KEY TERMS

Fill in the blanks below with the letters identifying the following concepts. Each concept is used one time only.

A.	Learning	Q.	Premack Principle
B.	Stimulus	R.	Aversive stimulus
C.	Behavioral theories	S.	Shaping
D.	Cognitive theories	T.	Reverse chaining
E.	Unconditioned stimulus	U.	Extinction
F.	Unconditioned response	V.	Schedule of reinforcement
G.	Neutral stimulus	W.	Fixed-ratio
H.	Classical conditioning	X.	Variable-ratio
I.	Law of Effect	Y.	Fixed-interval
J.	Operant conditioning	Z.	Variable-interval
K.	Consequence	AA.	Antecedent stimuli
L.	Reinforcer	BB.	Discrimination
M.	Primary reinforcers	CC.	Generalization
N.	Secondary reinforcers	DD.	Modeling
O.	Positive reinforcement	EE.	Vicarious learning
P.	Negative reinforcement	FF.	Self-regulation

1. Following classical conditioning, the formerly _____ becomes a conditioned stimulus.

2. Cues for what behavior will be reinforced or punished are provided by _____.

3. A change in an individual resulting from experience is _____.

4. _____, the type emphasized in Skinner's work, involves the use of pleasant and unpleasant consequences to change behavior.

5. A form of shaping in which complex skills are taught "backwards" is _____.

6. When behaviors learned under one set of conditions are used in other situations _____ is said to occur.

7. Learning to respond to one stimulus but not to other similar stimuli is called _____.

8. The type of learning process studied by Pavlov is called _____.

9. A condition in the environment that evokes behavior is a(n) ____.

10. The predictability of reinforcers is determined by the _____ applied to the learner.

11. The _____ states that when a response is followed by a pleasurable effect, the likelihood of repeating that response in the future tends to increase.

12. A general term for a consequence that strengthens or increases the frequency of behavior is _____.

13. _____ is the disappearance of a response due to the withdrawal of reinforcement.

14. An unpleasant consequence that provokes attempts at escape is called a(n) _____.

15. _____ attempt to explain learning by focusing on mental processes of human beings.

16. The _____ schedule of reinforcement involves administering a reinforcer following an unpredictable number of responses.

17. The _____ schedule of reinforcement involves reinforcing the first response following a set time interval.

18. _____, such as money or grades, acquire positive value by being associated with _____, such as food, security, and warmth.

19. A condition that follows a behavior and affects its frequency of later occurring is a(n) _____.

20. Imitating other people's behavior is referred to as _____.

21. The presentation of a reinforcer following a response is _____, whereas the removal of a punisher (or something unpleasant) following the response is _____.

22. Taking charge of one's own behavior by setting performance standards and criteria for receiving reinforcement is _____.

23. The _____ schedule of reinforcement involves reinforcing the first correct response following unpredictable time intervals.

24. In Pavlov's experiment, the meat powder served as a(n) _____.

25. The _____, sometimes called "Grandma's Rule," involves making involvement in a desirable activity contingent upon performing an undesirable activity.

26. When Pavlov's dog salivated to the meat powder, it was emitting a(n) _____.

27. _____ attempt to explain learning by focusing on observable behaviors of humans and animals.

28. The _____ schedule of reinforcement involves administering a reinforcer following a set number of responses.

29. Guiding learners by reinforcing small steps that lead to desired goals is called _____.

30. Learning from watching others being rewarded or punished is _____.

COMPLETION QUESTIONS

1. Changes in behavior as individuals mature are accounted for by two major processes: _____ and _____.

2. An environmental property to which we react is a _____.

3. Observable processes such as answering questions are the subject of _____ theories.

4. Nonobservable mental processes, such as thinking, are the subject of _____ theories.

5. The process through which a previously neutral stimulus becomes capable of evoking a new response through its association with a natural stimulus for that response is _____.

6. The response evoked by the unconditioned stimulus is called the _____.

7. In Pavlov's experiment the meat powder served as the _____.

8. A child who is swimming is frightened by thunder, and thereafter is afraid of water. In this instance the neutral stimulus is _____.

9. A student who studies hard receives an "A" grade and a new car from her parents for such an excellent performance. According to Thorndike's _____, she will therefore be more likely to study hard for tests in the future.

10. The use of positive and negative circumstances to modify behavior is the basis of _____ conditioning.

11. A stimulus that strengthens behavior is a _____; one that weakens or decreases behavior is a _____.

12. Stimuli such as grades and money, which have acquired positive value, are called _____ reinforcers.

13. The removal of an unpleasant condition following a behavior is _____.

14. A teacher says "Put your materials away neatly and then we'll play a game." This strategy is an example of the _____.

15. The removal of pleasant consequences following a response represents a form of punishment called _____.

16. _____ involves reinforcing learners for <u>approaching</u> the desired final behavior by having them learn parts of it at a time.

17. The process through which learned behavior is weakened by withdrawing reinforcement is _____.

18. The schedule of reinforcement which reinforces every correct response is called a _____ schedule.

19. _____ schedules dispense reinforcement on the basis of the number of responses emitted; _____ schedules dispense reinforcement on the basis of time.

20. The specific schedule of reinforcement that underlies gambling activities such as playing slot machines is the _____ schedule.

21. Pop quizzes given in a course impose a _____ schedule of reinforcement over students.

22. Antecedent stimuli are also known as _____, because they provide a signal or hint of what behaviors will be reinforced or punished.

23. A pigeon who learns to peck at a large disk but not at a small one has evidently learned _____.

24. Learning to stop at a stop sign generally transfers to all stop signs, even if exact sizes and street locations should differ. Such learning is an example of _____.

25. Learning by seeing others reinforced or punished for certain behaviors is called _____ learning.

26. A process in which individuals assume responsibility for monitoring and controlling their own behaviors is _____.

27. Relative to behavioral learning theory, _____ places a much greater emphasis on internal mental processes and learning from others.

MULTIPLE CHOICE

1. Which of the following best illustrates learning?

   a. Withdrawing your hand from a hot stove
   b. Avoiding a dog who is sitting by the road
   c. Blinking your eye when smoke is blown into it
   d. Wanting to eat when you are hungry.

2. Operant conditioning differs from classical conditioning by

   a. focusing on animal behavior to a much greater extent than human behavior.
   b. dealing mostly with reflexive types of responses.
   c. focusing on the relationship between behavior and its consequences.
   d. treating learners as passive rather than active agents.

3. Thorndike's Law of Effect stated that

   a. the last response made to a stimulus becomes the one most likely to be made when that stimulus is present again.
   b. the more a response is practiced the greater the proficiency at making that response becomes.
   c. if a response is followed by something satisfying, its likelihood of being repeated increases.
   d. it is merely the association in time between a stimulus and response, not reinforcement, that causes conditioning.

4. As Jill recites her answers to the history homework assignment, her teacher ridicules her for "not paying attention or being careful in her work." The next day Jill begins to tremble when it is time to review history homework again. Which of the following is most clearly illustrated in this example?

   a. Negative reinforcement
   b. Discrimination learning
   c. Operant conditioning
   d. Classical conditioning

5. In the above example (Item 4), "history homework" became a(n) _____ for anxiety.

   a. unconditioned stimulus
   b. primary reinforcer
   c. negative reinforcer
   d. conditioned stimulus

6. Which of the following is a primary reinforcer for a person who desires it?

   a. A ten dollar bill
   b. A cold drink
   c. A grade of "A"
   d. All of the above

7. Which of the following illustrates a correct application of the Premack Principle?

   a. "Comb your hair and then you can eat your ice cream."
   b. "Eat your lunch or I'll box your ears."
   c. "If I let you play for an hour, do you promise that you'll do your homework?
   d. "Watch how nicely your brother eats his oysters. Now, can you do the same?"

8. After mowing the grass, Frank is congratulated by his father who says, "Great going! You can forget about having to weed the garden for doing such a good job." Frank has received

   a. positive reinforcement.
   b. Punishment I.
   c. Punishment II.
   d. negative reinforcement.

9. Jamie hands in a very hastily done and sloppy homework assignment. She receives the low grade of D- for her effort. Jamie has been given

   a. positive reinforcement.
   b. Punishment I.
   c. Punishment II.
   d. negative reinforcement.

10. After calling Mathew a bad name, Andre is not allowed to go to the circus. He has received

   a. positive reinforcement.
   b. Punishment I.
   c. Punishment II.
   d. negative reinforcement.

11. Which of the following strategies for using punishment do most behavioral learning theorists favor?

   a. It should not be used with young children, regardless of the circumstances.
   b. Physical punishment should be used when other forms do not work.
   c. Make the number of punishments (reprimands) given in a class roughly equal to the number of rewards.
   d. Resort to punishment only when reinforcement strategies have failed.

12. Which of the following represents sound practical advice for teachers based on the principle of <u>immediacy of consequences?</u>

   a. Provide individual feedback immediately to all of your students.
   b. Wait at least a few days after a test to return papers to allow the experience and content tested to sink in.
   c. If a punishment is necessary, administer it as soon as possible after the misbehavior occurs.
   d. Begin a behavior modification program with long delays between response and reinforcement; then gradually decrease the delay period as behavior improves over time.

13. Whenever Alice fails to turn in homework, the teacher has her stay after school and do it then. However, the "personal" session with the teacher after school proves to be very reinforcing to Alice. Consequently, she becomes progressively less inclined to do her homework. Use of extinction to correct this problem would specifically involve

a. administering additional punishment for future offenses.
b. putting Alice on a reinforcement schedule for successfully completing homework.
c. using students who have completed homework as effective role models.
d. not giving Alice personal sessions when she fails to complete her homework.

14. Mr Burch, Alice's father, hates sending in his income tax form every year, but constantly worries that his return will be the "one" selected for auditing. Thus, he completes it honestly so that he won't get fined. The reinforcement schedule that Mr. Burch is (unknowingly) worried about each year is

a. fixed ratio.
b. variable ratio.
c. variable interval.
d. fixed interval.

15. A fiction writer keeps writing new manuscripts and sending them to book companies for review. She knows that some manuscripts may not make it, but, with the right conditions, any one could turn out to be a best seller. The reinforcement schedule under which she is working is the

a. fixed ratio.
b. variable ratio.
c. variable interval.
d. fixed interval.

16. Which types of reinforcement schedules tend to elicit the highest rates of responding and the greatest resistance to extinction?

a. Variable ratio and variable interval schedules
b. Variable interval and fixed interval schedules
c. Variable ratio and fixed ratio schedules
d. Fixed ratio and fixed interval schedules

17. A student loves to raise his hand and participate in friendly Mr. Foster's class. So when he attends mean Ms. Mendoza's class, he immediately starts doing the same. Such behavior is an example of _____ learning.

    a. discrimination
    b. generalization
    c. antecedent stimulus
    d. vicarious

18. As the similarity between two stimulus settings increases,

    a. generalization and discrimination both become easier.
    b. generalization becomes easier but discrimination becomes harder.
    c. generalization becomes harder but discrimination becomes easier.
    d. both generalization and discrimination become harder.

19. The correct sequence of Bandura's four phases is

    a. motivational, attentional, retention, and reproduction.
    b. motivational, attentional, reproduction, and retention.
    c. attentional, motivational, reproduction, and retention.
    d. attentional, retention, reproduction, and motivational.

20. In Bandura's classic study on modeling, ıildren who observed a film showing an aggressive adult being punished

    a. engaged in significantly fewer aggressive acts during subsequent play.
    b. appeared unaffected by the film during subsequent play.
    c. engaged in significantly more aggressive acts in subsequent play.
    d. showed less desire to see movies in later classes.

<u>APPLICATION:</u> Conditioning

A. A student in your second grade class, Scott, continually pushes other students and talks while in line. Using the behavioral principles you have learned, describe how you might teach him to follow the correct procedure (being quiet and orderly), <u>without</u> having to use any type of "severe" punishment. Since you cannot be certain that your first intervention will work, present a plan of action indicating several strategies that might be tried in sequence if earlier ones fail.

B. While Undrea is swinging on the parallel bars in physical education class, she loses her grip, slips, and falls with a loud thud. Undrea is hurt and horrified. The next day the mere sight of the parallel bars makes her feel extremely anxious. She refuses to go near them. The balance beam produces a similar reaction, though not as severe. She finally settles on tumbling exercises and spends the whole period doing those, far away from the threatening apparatus.

Discuss Undrea's experiences by identifying where each of the following occurred:

1. Classical conditioning
2. Unconditioned response
3. Unconditioned stimulus
4. Conditioned response
5. Unconditioned stimulus
6. Stimulus generalization
7. Stimulus discrimination

C. In teaching a fourth-grade class, you are concerned by the frequent episodes of loud talking and shouting. You decide that you'd like to establish a signal, such as turning out the lights, that will "automatically" evoke quiet. Describe how you might accomplish this. Which conditioning model, classical or operant, would be primarily involved?

D. Think of an applied classroom situation and identify at least two examples of teacher uses of each of the following:

1. Negative reinforcement
2. Positive reinforcement
3. Punishment I
4. Punishment II

APPLICATION: Schedules of Reinforcement

Suppose that you assist a teacher who wants to use a token economy system in her class. The system involves reinforcing good behavior with tokens that students can trade in at the end of the week for rewards or privileges. Give a specific example of how each of the following schedules might be used in dispensing the tokens. Also indicate your impressions about the relative effectiveness (possible advantages and disadvantages) of using that schedule.

1. fixed interval
2. fixed ratio
3. variable interval
4. variable ratio

APPLICATION: Modeling

Little Fred steps up to the plate wearing his Little League uniform and adjusts his stance in the exact same way as "Coot" Cutler, the local college baseball star. Fred pulls his left trouser leg sideways three times, digs both feet into the dirt, holds his bat far behind his left shoulder and points it at the pitcher twice, all in perfect Coot Cutler style. Fred is even batting left-handed (although he's naturally right-handed) since Coot is a switch-hitter and bats left-handed in opposing a right-handed pitcher.

Discuss Little Fred's behavior from the perspective of social learning theory. Use the following specific stages as a framework for describing how that behavior might have evolved:

1. Attentional
2. Retention
3. Reproduction
4. Motivational

ESSAY/DISCUSSION

1. Differentiate between behavioral and cognitive approaches to learning. What, in your opinion, can each offer today's teachers that would help them understand student behavior in their classrooms?

2. Define what is meant by "learning," and explain to what extent that definition appears applicable to each of the following:

   a. learning to walk
   b. learning to talk
   c. favoring certain foods over others
   d. favoring certain people over others

3. Analyze the relative effectiveness of reinforcement and punishment as components of operant conditioning. Also define and differentiate between positive reinforcement, negative reinforcement, Punishment I, and Punishment II. If punishment were necessary in a classroom situation, which of the two types might you generally favor? Why?

4. Television programming is frequently criticized for the high incidence of violence featured. Discuss the possible dangers of TV violence in reference to social learning theory and Bandura's work on modeling.

5. After hearing you describe some conditioning principles, a teacher acquaintance says, "That conditioning stuff seems o.k. for animals, but it is dehumanizing and manipulative with children." Describe your views on this issue concerning the ethics of using operant conditioning in classrooms.

ANSWERS

Matching Warm-Ups

Quiz 1	Quiz 2	Quiz 3	Quiz 4
a. 4 (93)	a. 4 (97)	a. 1 (110)	a. 4 (95)
b. 3 (93)	b. 3 (97)	b. 4 (109)	b. 3 (116)
c. 1 (93)	c. 1 (100)	c. 2 (108)	c. 4 (95)
d. 2 (93)	d. 2 (100)	d. 5 (110)	d. 1 (95)
			e. 3 (116-117)
			f. 2 (93)
			g. 3 (116-120)
			h. 4 (95)
			i. 1 (95)

Key Terms

1.	G (94)	11.	I (95)	21.	O,P (97)
2.	AA (114)	12.	L (97)	22.	FF (118)
3.	A (92)	13.	U (106)	23.	Z (110)
4.	J (95)	14.	R (100)	24.	E (93)
5.	T (104)	15.	D (93)	25.	Q (99)
6.	CC (115)	16.	X (109)	26.	F (93)
7.	BB (115)	17.	Y (110)	27.	C (93)
8.	H (94)	18.	N;M (97)	28.	W (108)
9.	B (93)	19.	K (96)	29.	S (103)
10.	V (108)	20.	DD (116)	30.	EE (117)

Completion Questions

1. learning; development (92)
2. stimulus (93)
3. behavioral (93)
4. cognitive (93)
5. classical conditioning (94)
6. unconditioned response (93)
7. unconditioned stimulus (93)
8. water (93-94)
9. Law of Effect (94)
10. operant (95)
11. reinforcer; punisher (96)
12. secondary (97)
13. negative reinforcement (97)
14. Premack Principle (99)
15. Punishment II (100)
16. shaping (103)
17. extinction (106)
18. continuous (108)
19. ratio; interval (108-110)
20. variable-ratio (109)
21. variable-interval (110)
22. cues (114)
23. discrimination (115)
24. generalization (115)
25. vicarious (117)
26. self-regulation (118)
27. social learning theory (116)

Multiple-Choice

1.	b (92)	11.	d (101)
2.	c (95)	12.	c (102-103)
3.	c (94)	13.	d (106)
4.	d (93-94)	14.	c (110)
5.	d (93)	15.	b (109)
6.	b (97)	16.	a (110,112)
7.	a (99)	17.	b (115-116)
8.	d (97)	18.	b (115)
9.	b (100)	19.	d (116-117)
10.	c (100)	20.	a (118)

5 Information Processing and Memory

CHAPTER OUTLINE

I. Humans as Information Processors

II. Information Processing
   A. Sensory Register
      1. Information is received and held for short periods of time
      2. Sperling's experiments
      3. Implications of sensory registers
      4. Perception
      5. Gestalt Psychology
         a. Meaning of "Gestalt"
         b. Closure
         c. Figure-ground relationship
      6. Attention
      7. Gaining attention
   B. Teachers on teaching: Focusing on important information
   C. Short-term memory
      1. Holds limited information for a few seconds
      2. Role of rehearsal
      3. Capacity is believed to be 5-7 "bits"
   D. Long-term memory
      1. Large capacity, possible permanent storage
      2. Episodic, semantic, and procedural memory
   E. Levels of processing
      1. Theory and research
      2. Dual code theory of memory

F. Allocating mental resources
   1. Automatization
   2. Transfer appropriate processing
G. Teachers on teaching: Helping students process information
H. Forgetting
   1. Interference
      a. Retroactive inhibition
      b. Proactive inhibition
      c. Proactive facilitation
      d. Retroactive facilitation
I. Primacy and recency effects
J. Theory into practice: Reducing retroactive inhibition
   1. Separate materials in time
   2. Use different methods
   3. Ensure mastery of material

III. Memory Strategies
A. Verbal learning
   1. Paired-associate learning
   2. Serial learning
   3. Free-recall learning
B. Paired-associate learning
   1. Importance of stimulus discrimination
   2. Stimulus selection
   3. Stimulus coding
C. Theory into practice: Paired-associate learning strategies
   1. Imagery
   2. Keyword method
   3. Yodai mnemonics
D. Serial and free-recall learning
E. Theory into practice: Serial and free-recall learning strategies
   1. Organization
   2. Loci method
   3. Pegword method
   4. Rhyming
   5. Initial-letter strategies
F. Practice
   1. Massed versus distributed practice
   2. Part learning
   3. Overlearning
G. Teachers on teaching: Overlearning and memorization

Summary/Study Questions/Suggested Readings

CHAPTER OBJECTIVES

1. List the three major components of memory and describe the role that each plays in the processing of information.
2. Describe the two ways that our long-term memory codes information.

3. Describe why we remember things that we study thoroughly better than things to which we pay little attention.
4. Describe how information can be presented so as to decrease the chance that it will be forgotten.
5. Use memory strategies to remember lists of information and pairs of facts.
6. Explain the advantages of distributed practice over massed practice.

MATCHING WARM-UPS

Match the numbers of the descriptions on the right to the corresponding items on the left. A given item from the right column may be used more than once or not at all.

Quiz 1: Types of Memory

_____ a.	Sensory register	1. Recollection of personal events
_____ b.	Short-term memory	2. Knowledge of how to write or jump
_____ c.	Episodic long-term	3. Very rapid decay
_____ d.	Semantic long-term	4. Our acquired knowledge
_____ e.	Procedural long-term	5. Rehearsal prevents loss

Quiz 2: Forgetting

_____ a.	Retroactive interference	1. Skill 2 helps Skill 1
_____ b.	Retroactive facilitation	2. Skill 1 helps Skill 2
_____ c.	Proactive interference	3. Skill 2 hinders Skill 1
_____ d.	Proactive facilitation	4. Skill 1 hinders Skill 2

Quiz 3: Learning Strategies

_____ a.	Keyword method	1. Using a rhyming scheme for serial recall
_____ b.	Loci method	2. Forming images of mathematical operations
_____ c.	Yodai mnemonics	3. Memorizing while being hypnotized
_____ d.	Pegword	4. Imagining list items in different familiar locations
		5. Linking paired-associates through imagery

Quiz 4: Notable Names

_____ a. model of information processing
_____ b. sensory register recall
_____ c. Gestalt psychology movement
_____ d. episodic and semantic memories
_____ e. levels-of-processing theory
_____ f. dual code theory of memory
_____ g. classic experiment on interference
_____ h. electrical stimulation of brain
_____ i. overlearning
_____ j. transfer-appropriate processing

1. Bransford
2. Paivio
3. Tulving
4. Krueger
5. Sperling
6. Atkinson & Shiffrin
7. Thorndike
8. Peterson
9. Wertheimer
10. Penfield
11. Craik & Lockhart

KEY TERMS

Fill in the blanks below with the letters identifying the following concepts. Each concept is used one time only.

A. Information processing perspective
B. Sensory register
C. Perception
D. Gestalt psychology
E. Closure
F. Figure-ground relationship
G. Attention
H. Short-term memory
I. Long-term memory
J. Rehearsal
K. Episodic memory
L. Semantic memory
M. Procedural memory
N. Schemata
O. Automatization
P. Levels of processing theory
Q. Dual coding theory of memory
R. Transfer-appropriate processing
S. Interference
T. Retroactive inhibition
U. Proactive inhibition
V Proactive facilitation
W. Retroactive facilitation
X. Primacy effect
Y. Recency effect
Z. Verbal learning
AA. Paired-associate learning
BB. Serial learning
CC. Free-recall learning
DD. Stimulus selection
EE. Stimulus coding
FF. Mnemonics
GG. Imagery
HH. Keyword method
II. Yodai mnemonics
JJ. Loci method
KK. Pegword method
LL. Massed practice
MM. Distributed practice
NN. Part learning
OO. Overlearning

1. The process through which tasks can be performed using little effort or direct attention is _____.

2. An imagery strategy, developed by the Japanese, for helping students to learn math operations is _____.

3. The process of interpreting stimuli received by the senses is called _____.

4. Words appearing at the beginning of a list are recalled more easily than others due to the _____.

5. Memories of concepts, principles, rules, and information are stored in long-term _____.

6. Mentally organized networks of connected ideas are called _____.

7. When new learning is beneficial to performance on previously learned tasks, _____ is said to occur.

8. The idea that memory is partly dependent on the similarity between acquisition and recall conditions is emphasized by the _____ theory.

9. Memories of personal experiences are stored in long-term _____.

10. The strategy of continuing to practice material that is already well-learned is called _____.

11. A strategy for learning paired-associates by focusing on certain aspects of the stimulus words, such as their initial letters, is _____.

12. _____ is considered to have almost limitless capacity for storing information over time.

13. An effective memorization strategy which involves picturing items in one's mind is mental _____.

14. _____ involves connecting response members with stimulus members.

15. When a new task interferes with previously learned skills, _____ is said to occur.

16. According to the _____, information in long-term memory is stored in visual and verbal forms.

17. Words appearing at the end of a list are recalled more easily than others due to the _____.

18. A strategy for remembering lists by picturing items in familiar locations is called _____.

19. _____ has been defined as involving three aspects: alertness, selectivity, and concentration.

20. Learning a list of facts in any order represents _____.

21. Trying to learn an entire task in relatively few sessions represents _____, whereas trying to learn smaller parts of the task over a greater period of time represents _____.

22. Perceiving certain parts of an object to stand out relative to others is a manifestation of the _____.

23. _____ occurs when involvement with certain stimuli distracts you from concentrating on other stimuli.

24. Perceiving an object as whole even though pieces of the object are missing illustrates the principle of _____.

25. Cognitive psychologists take a(n) _____ in studying how knowledge is absorbed and used by human beings.

26. A general strategy for learning paired-associates which may use mnenomics, keywords, or imagery for associating items is _____.

27. The mental repetition of information to facilitate retention is called _____.

28. A strategy for improving memory of paired-associates by linking pair members through imagery is called _____.

29. A strategy for serial learning in which facts are linked to known words through vivid imagery is called _____.

30. _____ is the acquisition of facts and general knowledge from oral and written presentations.

31. Knowledge of how to perform physical tasks is stored in long-term _____.

32. How we recognize forms and configurations was an emphasis of the _____ movement in Germany.

33. Learning one subskill of a complex task at a time represents _____.

34. When previous learning is beneficial to the acquisition of new skills, _____ is said to occur.

35. The place in the memory system where information is initially received and held for a very short time is the _____.

36. The memory system that holds a limited amount of information for a few seconds is _____.

37. Learning a list of facts in a specified sequence represents _____.

38. According to the _____, the more mental attention we give to a stimulus, the greater the likelihood we will remember it.

39. When previously learned skills interfere with learning on subsequent tasks, _____ is said to occur.

40. A general term for special methods designed to facilitate memory is _____.

COMPLETION QUESTIONS

1. The theory that concerns the study of how information is attended to, processed, and retrieved is _____.

2. The component of the memory system that initially receives incoming information is the _____.

3. A German word meaning "form" or "configuration" is _____.

4. When your test paper is returned, the grade of "A" stands out for you, while you fail to notice other stimuli such as the instructor's comments. This illustrates the perceptual phenomenon of _____ relationship.

5. The process of trying to maintain information in short-term memory is called _____.

6. According to Miller (1967), short-term memory has a capacity of five to _____ bits of information.

7. The memory system that can hold a limited amount of information for a few seconds is _____.

8. The three parts of long-term memory are _____, which contains memories of personal experiences; _____, which contains memories of acquired knowledge and information; and _____, which contains knowledge of how to do things.

9. A cognitive framework that individuals use to organize and interrelate knowledge and experiences is called a(n)_____.

10. Juan rides his 10-speed bicycle skillfully, shifting gears and keeping perfect balance, without having to think about his actions. This behavior illustrates the process of _____.

11. According to the _____ theory, the more a stimulus is attended to and processed, the more likely it is to be remembered.

12. The dual code theory of memory proposes that information is stored in long-term memory in _____ and _____ forms.

13. A student who has learned French finds it much easier to learn Spanish. This example illustrates _____.

14. A student in a statistics course receives high grades on every exam, but finds himself unable to interpret the same statistical concepts when reading a journal article. This is explained by the theory of _____.

15. A student who is learning how to sail finds that he now better understands some of the principles he formerly learned in a class on surfing. This example illustrates _____.

16. A student who has learned the rules for conduct in his former teacher's class is finding it difficult to learn the somewhat different rules in his new teacher's class. This example illustrates _____.

17. The type of task in which the learner tries to link members of one list of words with members of another list is called _____ learning.

18. _____ learning involves memorizing a list without concern about order or sequence.

19. _____ learning involves memorizing a list in a specified order.

20. Clara remembers the French words "jeune fille," for "young girl," by forming a mental image of girl sitting on a horse (filly) on a summer (June) day. She is using the _____ method of remembering.

21. The _____ method involves imaging objects in familiar locations, whereas the _____ method involves imaging the objects with familiar words contained in a rhyme.

22. Memorizing the sentence "Every good boy does fine" to remember the musical notes, E,G,B,D, and F illustrates the _____ strategy.

23. _____ practice is generally effective for retention, since it allows new information to be integrated with long-term memory over time.

24. Answering this very question day after day even though you get it right (hopefully) this very first trial would represent use of the _____ strategy for remembering.

MULTIPLE-CHOICE

Select the best answer for each of the following items.

1. You haven't tried roller skating in years, but are invited to a good friend's party at the local skating rink. You expect to immediately fall on your face, but surprisingly, get back in the old groove very fast. Which memory system is being used?

   a. Semantic long-term
   b. Episodic long-term
   c. Procedural long-term
   d. Short-term

2. You are shown a math problem to solve. As you try to remember the formula involved, which memory system is being searched?

   a. Semantic long-term
   b. Procedural long-term
   c. Episodic long-term
   d. Short-term

3. One night you start thinking about that wild party your high school friend had when his parents were away for the weekend. Images of the other people who attended and some of their escapades come to mind. Which memory system is being searched?

   a. Semantic long-term
   b. Sensory register
   c. Episodic long-term
   d. Short-term

4. As you sit at your desk, a figure comes into view. You look at him, but are still unaware of his exact features and identity. Which memory system is involved at this moment?

   a. Semantic long-term
   b. Sensory register
   c. Episodic long-term
   d. Short-term

5. You are lost in a strange town and are told by a stranger to "go three blocks, turn right, then go one block, turn left, go to the second traffic light and turn right." Which memory system will become most significant in trying to remember this information as you drive?

   a. Procedural long-term
   b. Sensory register
   c. Episodic long-term
   d. Short-term

6. Modern day educational psychologists take an information-processing perspective in studying

   a. human learning.
   b. animal learning.
   c. behavior modification techniques.
   d. all of the above.

7. Which of the following statements about perception is <u>false?</u>

   a. What is perceived may vary depending upon the learner's motivation.
   b. Perception has essentially the same meaning as reception.
   c. Perception can be defined as the interpretation of stimuli.
   d. We often perceive things not as they really are, but according to what we think they are.

8. Which of the following perceptions might be directly explained by the principle of figure-ground relationship?

   a. You glance at the sun, close your eyes, and continue to perceive its image.
   b. You remember yourself as highly articulate and confident at your first job interview even though you were quite the opposite.
   c. In searching your lawn for the house keys that you dropped, you fail to notice the snake slithering in direct view.
   d. You look at your nearly empty refrigerator and envision a large turkey, a roast, a six pack of beer, and a layer cake.

9. Long-term memory is believed by theorists to be

   a. mostly visual in nature.
   b. an exact copy of the input information.
   c. relatively susceptible to decay.
   d. mostly semantic in nature.

10. Schemata consist of

    a. frameworks for organizing ideas in semantic memory.
    b. recall strategies through which episodic memory is searched for specific information.
    c. strategies or game plans for solving problems.
    d. incomplete images or cues that our perceptions shape into whole objects.

11. Based on the dual coding theory, which of the following learning strategies should be most effective for remembering a new object?

a. Seeing it and touching it
b. Naming it and then rehearsing the name
c. Seeing it and naming it
d. Viewing it at different locations in a room

12. Retroactive inhibition occurs when

a. prior learning interferes with new learning.
b. new learning interferes with prior learning.
c. prior learning facilitates acquisition of new information.
d. new learning improves performance on previously learned tasks.

13. Which of the following illustrates proactive facilitation?

a. Billy finds that knowing Latin hinders his learning of Russian.
b. As Mike studies chemistry he finds that his understanding of cooking is improving.
c. Barbara finds statistics very easy as a result of having taken an algebra course the year before.
d. Geri learns to operate her new VCR, and then discovers she has forgotten how to work her stereo taping system.

14. Student A takes French from Ms. Bovier who places emphasis on learning vocabulary and grammatical rules. Student B takes French from Mr. Knox who emphasizes its conversational use. Based on the theory of transfer appropriate processing

a. Student A will know more vocabulary and grammatical rules.
b. Student B will be better at using French in everyday conversation.
c. both a. and b.
d. none of the above.

15. Select the method that is not recommended for reducing retroactive inhibition. If all are recommended, pick response d.

a. Teach two similar concepts by alternating between them. Teach a little about one, then a little about the other, and so on.
b. Present one concept using one teaching method and the similar concept using a different teaching method.
c. Use frequent assessments of student's understanding and reteaching if mastery is not achieved.
d. All are recommended.

16. A student is asked to learn the names of the United States presidents in the order in which they held office. This is an example of

a. paired-associate learning.
b. free-recall learning.
c. part learning.
d. serial learning.

17. A student memorizes the names of 10 pizza restaurants in his town. This is an example of

a. paired-associate learning.
b. free-recall learning.
c. part learning.
d. serial learning.

18. A boy tries to remember the titles of different books by imaging characters from each book in a different room of his house (e.g., Moby Dick in his bathtub). The specific memory strategy being used is the _____ method.

a. pegword
b. keyword
c. loci
d. Yodai mnemonics

19. You see a fellow student walking down the hall reciting "One-bun, Two-shoe...Ten-hen." She says she is using that recital to remember words. Which types of words are probably involved?

a. Words that begin with the same letter as the pegwords (bun, shoe, etc.)
b. The pegwords (bun, shoe, etc.) themselves
c. Words mentally imaged in association with the pegwords
d. Words mentally imaged in association with the numbers ("one," "two," etc.)

20. Which of the following is true?

a. Overlearning produces inhibition or fatigue effects, thereby depressing performance.
b. Distributed practice is generally recommended over massed practice.
c. Massed practice means essentially the same thing as overlearning.
d. Part learning usually increases retroactive inhibition between items on a long list.

APPLICATION: Short-Term Memory

This exercise can be used to assess your or another person's short-term memory capacity. The examiner should tell the subject to "listen to the following set of digits and then when I say, 'Go,' write the digits in the exact order of presentation." Repeat the procedure for each set, being sure to announce the digits clearly and loudly. Here is a sample group.

Set 1: 8, 6, 1, 4
2: 9, 5, 8, 2, 5
3: 10, 1, 3, 8, 5, 2
4: 7, 4, 1, 3, 7, 5, 4
5: 8, 2, 6, 8, 9, 1, 10, 3
6: 2, 6, 3, 10, 2, 4, 9, 5, 6

A. How do your (or the other person's) results compare with Miller's estimate (see text) of short-term memory capacity?
B. For more reliable data, test several people on this task. What appears to be a typical performance?
C. Try the same test, but ask the subjects to recall the digits in reverse order. How do the results compare with those obtained above? If there is a difference, what do you feel accounts for it?

APPLICATION: Long-Term Memory

Explore the longevity of long-term retention by answering (or asking others to answer) the following four questions.

I. What did you eat for dinner yesterday?
II. What did you eat for dinner one week ago?
III. What did you eat for dinner last July 22?
IV. What did you eat for dinner last December 25?

The speed of, and degree of confidence, in responses are likely to vary for these questions. Explain why, discussing the differences between the search and retrieval processes involved. Finally, identify which memory system, episodic or semantic, would be the focus of that search. (Possibly unhelpful hint: it's a different system from the one you are presently searching to answer this question.)

APPLICATION: Interference

A. Think of each of the following applied learning situations and indicate, based on your experiences or intuitions, whether the predominant effects would be, a) retroactive inhibition, b) retroactive facilitation, c) proactive inhibition, d) proactive facilitation, or e) some combination. Explain your answers.

1. You learn to ride a bicycle using training wheels; then switch to one without training wheels.
2. You learn the commands for one computer system (e.g., IBM) and then learn the commands for a second computer system (e.g., Apple).
3. You learn to drive an automatic-shift car and then learn to drive a manual-shift car.
4. You learn to play racquetball and then learn to play tennis.
5. You learn to type on a conventional typewriter and then learn to use a word-processor.
6. A child learns to print letters and then learns cursive writing.
7. A child learns addition and then learns subtraction.

B. After completing the above exercise, consider your own teaching area and identify one example in which each of the inhibition-facilitation outcomes (a-d) seems likely to occur. Where inhibition is predicted, discuss your ideas for a teaching strategy that could minimize its effects.

APPLICATION: Paired-Associate Learning

Test different people on learning each of the following three lists by (a) first showing the stimulus and response words together and (b) then showing only the stimulus words and asking them to supply the responses. Write the learning and test list items on index cards so that you can vary their order each trial. How many trials are needed on the average to achieve a perfect performance on each? If there are differences across lists, explain why you think they occurred.

List A		List B		List C	
Stim	Resp	Stim	Resp	Stim	Resp
TYW	BOY	TAW	BOY	TOW	BOY
FML	PIG	FAL	PIG	FLAG	PIG
CDP	BOAT	CIP	BOAT	CAP	BOAT
MNP	HOUSE	MIP	HOUSE	MAP	HOUSE
LBD	BALL	LUD	BALL	LID	BALL
TYP	WATCH	TED	WATCH	TOP	WATCH

APPLICATION: Memory Strategies

A. Use the keyword method to learn List C in the previous exercise. Which pairs seem easier to learn that way? Why?

B. Explain what would be involved in learning the response words only in List C using each of the following:

1. loci method
2. pegword method
3. rhyming method
4. initial letter strategy

C. Which method(s) would be effective for <u>serial</u> as opposed to free-recall learning?

COMPUTER EXERCISE

The EDUCATIONAL PSYCHOLOGY COMPUTER DISK for this text contains a program called FREE RECALL. It allows you to experience some of the phenomena regarding learning and memory discussed in this chapter. The specific task it presents asks you to recall as many words as you can from a list of 18 words. You can vary the type of word (nonsense, abstract, or concrete), the exposure interval for each word, and the number of trials allowed to master the list. Following each recall trial, you receive an analysis of which words you correctly identified, which you omitted, and which you "made up" (i.e., do not appear on the program's list). You also receive an analysis of your recall score for the beginning of the list (primacy effect), middle, and end (recency effect). The User's Guide presents complete descriptions and a variety of exercises for exploring memory principles by testing yourself and others.

ESSAY/DISCUSSION

1. Define what is meant by "information-processing perspective" and discuss how this perspective differs from behavioral orientations to learning.

2. Describe theorists' conceptions about each of the following memory systems with regard to capacity, duration, and retrieval strategies: sensory register, short-term memory, and long-term memory.

3. Describe what is meant by retroactive inhibition. Identify and discuss strategies that teachers can use to reduce retroactive inhibition in presenting or assigning instructional materials to students.

4. The levels-of-processing theory and the dual-code theory of memory are two accepted models of information processing. Describe each and discuss your views about its major implications for teaching practices (i.e., for increasing students' retention of information). Identify examples of teaching strategies that would incorporate each of these approaches.

5. Identify at least five memory strategies that can be used to improve performance on paired-associate or recall tasks. Evaluate and compare them based on your judgment of <u>effectiveness</u> and <u>practicality.</u> That is, which strategies do you feel are more useful than others? Explain your answers.

ANSWERS

Matching Warm-Ups

Quiz 1	Quiz 2	Quiz 3	Quiz 4
a. 3 (127)	a. 3 (139)	a. 5 (147)	a. 6 (127)
b. 5 (130)	b. 1 (141)	b. 4 (148)	b. 5 (127)
c. 1 (134)	c. 4 (139)	c. 2 (148)	c. 9 (129)
d. 4 (134)	d. 2 (141)	d. 1 (149)	d. 3 (134)
e. 2 (134)			e. 11 (136)
			f. 2 (136)
			g. 8 (139)
			h. 10 (142)
			i. 4 (151)
			j. 1 (138)

Key Terms

1. O (137)	21. LL;MM (151)
2. II (148)	22. F (128)
3. C (127)	23. S (139)
4. X (142)	24. E (128)
5. L (134)	25. A (127)
6. N (135)	26. EE (146)
7. W (141)	27. J (130)
8. R (138)	28. HH (147)
9. K (134)	29. KK (149)
10. OO (151)	30. Z (144)
11. DD (146)	31. M (134)
12. I (130)	32. D (128)
13. GG (146)	33. NN (151)
14. AA (145)	34. V (141)
15. T (139)	35. B (127)
16. Q (136)	36. H (130)
17. Y (142)	37. BB (145)
18. JJ (148)	38. P (136)
19. G (129)	39. U (139)
20. CC (145)	40. FF (146)

Completion Questions

1. information processing theory (127)
2. sensory register (127)
3. Gestalt (128)
4. figure-ground (128)
5. rehearsal (130)
6. seven (132)
7. short-term (130)
8. episodic; semantic; procedural (134)
9. schema (135)
10. automatization (137)
11. levels-of-processing (136)
12. verbal; visual (136)
13. proactive facilitation (141)
14. transfer-appropriate processing (138)
15. retroactive facilitation (141)
16. proactive inhibition (139)
17. paired-associate (145)
18. free-recall (145)
19. serial (145)
20. keyword (147)
21. loci; pegword (148-149)
22. initial letter (150)
23. distributed (151)
24. overlearning (151)

Multiple-Choice

1. c (134)
2. a (134)
3. c (134)
4. b (127)
5. d (130)
6. a (127)
7. b (127)
8. c (128)
9. d (134)
10. a (135)
11. c (136)
12. b (139)
13. c (141)
14. c (138)
15. a (143)
16. d (145)
17. b (145)
18. c (148)
19. c (149)
20. b (151)

6 Meaningful Learning

CHAPTER OUTLINE

I. Making Information Meaningful
    A. Rote and meaningful learning
        1. Rote learning refers to memorization
        2. Meaningful learning involves linkage of information to previous knowledge
    B. Inert versus useful knowledge
    C. Schema theory and meaningful learning
    D. Helping students understand
    E. Advance organizers
    F. Teachers on teaching: Increasing the meaningfulness of learning
    G. Theory into practice: Advance organizers
    H. Organization of information
    I. Questions
        1. Influence "mathemagenic" behaviors
        2. Can occur prior to or after material and be factual or pharaphrased types
    J. Elaboration
    K. Generative learning
    L. Theory into practice: Study strategies
        1. SQ3R/SQ4R
        2. MURDER
        3. Cooperative scripts
    M. Metacognitive learning strategies
    N. Theory into practice: Reciprocal teaching

O. Teaching thinking skills
   1. Instrumental enrichment
   2. Research results

II. Study Strategies
   A. Underlining
   B. Note taking
   C. Summarizing
   D. Student-generated questions
   E. Outlining, networking, and mapping
   F. Cooperative scripts
   G. Effective study strategies: Conclusions
      1. Specificity
      2. Generativity
      3. Executive monitoring
      4. Personal efficacy

III. Concept Learning
   A. Teaching of concepts
      1. The rule-example-rule pattern is used by effective teachers
      2. Examples
   B. Teachers on Teaching: Teaching concepts

IV. Tranfer of Learning and Problem Solving
   A. Transfer of concepts
      1. Same context
      2. Varied context
   B. Teachers on teaching: Helping students transfer learning
   C. Strategies for solving problems
      1. Means-ends analysis
      2. Extracting relevant information
      3. Representing the problem
      4. Obstacles to problem solving
      5. Creative problem solving
   D. Teachers on teaching: Problem solving

V. Cognitive Models of Instruction
   A. Jerome Bruner: Discovery learning
   B. Theory into practice: Discovery learning
   C. Teachers on teaching: Discovery learning
   D. David Ausubel: Reception learning
      1. Phase One: Presentation of advance organizer
      2. Phase Two: Presentation of learning task or material
      3. Phase Three: Strengthening cognitive organization
   E. Theory into practice: Expository teaching

F. Robert Gagne: Events of learning and instruction
   1. Events of learning
   2. Events of instruction
   3. Relationship between events of learning and events of instruction

Summary/Study Questions/Suggested Readings

CHAPTER OBJECTIVES

1. Use advance organizers to help students understand new information.
2. Use and teach three strategies for understanding and remembering material in textbooks.
3. Describe steps to use when attempting to solve problems.
4. Describe how topics can be explored through the use of discovery learning.
5. Describe the advantages of reception learning and how teachers can most effectively use expository teaching.

MATCHING WARM-UPS

Match the numbers of the descriptions on the right to the corresponding items on the left. A given item from the right column may be used more than once or not at all.

Quiz 1: Gagne's Events of Instruction

_____	a. Motivation Phase	1. Overt demonstration
_____	b. Apprehending Phase	2. Task expectations
_____	c. Acquisition Phase	3. Transfer
_____	d. Retention Phase	4. Evaluation and consequences
_____	e. Recall Phase	5. Attention
_____	f. Generalization Phase	6. Linkage to prior knowledge
_____	g. Performance Phase	7. Into long-term memory
_____	h. Feedback Phase	8. Out of long-term memory

Quiz 2: Notable Names: Matching Quiz

_____	a. Functional fixedness	1. Ausubel
_____	b. Inert knowledge	2. Bruner
_____	c. Advance organizers	3. Duncker
_____	d. Discovery learning	4. Gagne
_____	e. Instructional Enrichment	5. Rothkopf
_____	f. Generative learning	6. Wittrock
_____	g. Events of learning	7. Robinson
_____	h. Expository teaching	8. Palincsar
_____	i. SQ4R	9. Feuerstein
_____	j. Mathemagenic behaviors	10. Bransford
_____	k. Reciprocal teaching	
_____	l. Events of instruction	

KEY TERMS

Fill in the blanks below with the letter identifying the following concepts. Each concept is used one time only.

A. Rote learning
B. Meaningful learning
C. Inert knowledge
D. Advance organizers
E. Mathemagenic behaviors
F. Elaboration
G. Generative learning
H. Cooperative scripts
I. Metacognitive strategies
J. SQ4R
K. Reciprocal teaching
L. Instructional enrichment
M. Rule-example-rule
N. Transfer of learning
O. Problem solving
P. Means-ends analysis
Q. Functional fixedness
R. Discovery learning
S. Reception learning
T. Expository teaching
U. Progressive differentiation
V. Deductive teaching approaches

1. Information learned in school that may have little application to real life situations is _____.

2. A systematic study strategy that involves surveying, questioning, reading, reflecting, reciting, and reviewing material is _____.

3. Relating new information to existing knowledge is referred to as _____.

4. A theory by Wittrock that emphasizes the active interaction of new learning with existing knowledge is _____.

5. General statements given before instruction to help students relate new information to existing knowledge are _____.

6. Determining the difference between the current state and the desired goal, and then systematically working toward that goal in substeps illustrates the _____ approach to problem solving.

7. Memorization of facts or associations is referred to as _____.

8. A program specifically designed to develop thinking skills in children is _____.

9. A method in which students learn meta-cognitive skills by thinking of questions, summarizing, predicting, and assuming the role of teacher while reading is _____.

10. Methods intended to make students aware of their own learning while studying materials are called _____.

11. The step-by-step movement from general concepts to specific information is called _____.

12. The presentation of information to students in an organized manner to engender meaningful learning is _____.

13. Learning that occurs when students listen to information presented by teachers is _____.

14. Beginning a lesson with general concepts and then gradually introducing specific examples is the strategy used in _____.

15. A study strategy in which students work in pairs and alternate summarizing materials is _____.

16. The inability to perceive new uses for familiar objects in problem solving is called _____.

17. Stating a definition, presenting instances, and then restating the definition is the pattern used in the _____ approach of teaching.

18. Applying skills in a new situation is called _____.

19. An instructional approach in which students learn from their own explorations with materials and concepts is _____.

20. The process of thinking about material to be learned in relation to one's own knowledge is called _____.

21. Activities that help people learn are _____.

22. The application of knowledge and skills to the achievement of specific goals is _____.

COMPLETION QUESTIONS

1. Ausubel's theory distinguishes between two types of learning, one involving memorization the other integration with present knowledge. They are _____ and _____.

2. Knowledge acquired in school that has little applicability to students' real-life experiences is called _____ knowledge.

3. According to _____ theory, information that can be fitted into existing mental frameworks is more easily understood, learned, and retained than information that cannot be so fitted.

4. Meaningful background or "mental scaffolding" to which new information can be related is established by _____.

5. Questioning, underlining, and elaborating are all examples of _____ behaviors which help a person learn.

6. Questions that use different words than those appearing in the text to emphasize the learning of meanings are called _____ questions.

7. In studying for the next test, John summarizes a section of the text while Maria listens and comments on her interpretation. Then they switch roles. They are using the _____ method of studying.

8. The component steps of the SQ4R method are survey, _____, read, _____, recite, and _____.

9. A tutoring orientation that uses teacher demonstration of comprehension-monitoring techniques and a four-part model to improve the reading skills of students is the _____ teaching method.

10. A program designed to build such intellectual skills as categorization, comparison, orientation in space, and numerical progressions is _____.

11. The component steps of the MURDER training program are _____, understand, _____, detect, _____, and review.

12. Categories into which specific elements can be grouped are called _____.

13. When a student uses previously learned information in a new, somewhat different situation _____ is said to occur.

14. The question "What is the difference between where I am now and where I want to be" is a fundamental step in the _____ approach to problem solving.

15. A student fails to perceive that a chalkboard eraser can also be used as a paperweight to keep papers from blowing while he closes the window. This block to problem solving is called _____.

16. An instructional approach in which students are encouraged to learn from their own activities and observations is _____ learning.

17. _____ teaching involves presenting well-organized, carefully sequenced information to students.

18. The step-by-step movement from general concepts to specific information, emphasizing contrasts between old and new concepts is called _____.

19. General ideas precede specific ideas in _____ teaching approaches.

20. In Gagne's scheme the first critical instructional event is to activate _____.

MULTIPLE-CHOICE

1. Meaningful learning can be described as

   a. involving arbitrary associations.
   b. involving verbatim memorization.
   c. the type of learning that most teachers naturally emphasize in their classes.
   d. relating new material to existing knowledge.

2. Schema theory assumes that information is stored in

   a. essentially the same structural composition in which it was presented.
   b. chronological order, based on the order in which it was received.
   c. order of its importance to the individual.
   d. hierarchies containing groupings of specific information.

3. The major rationale for advance organizers is the idea that

   a. reviewing lesson material increases motivation for learning that topic.
   b. learning is more effective when there is relevant background experiences to which new information can be related.
   c. providing additional practice serves as a form of overlearning that strengthens associations.
   d. lecture presentations become clearer if students have an outline listing the major topics.

4. Which of the following study activities would be considered a mathemagenic behavior?

   a. Answering questions
   b. Underlining
   c. Summarizing
   d. All of the above

5. Research shows that questions presented prior to the instructional material

   a. are detrimental to overall performance.
   b. improve overall performance.
   c. improve learning of question-related material but hinder incidental learning.
   d. hinder learning of question-related material, but improve incidental learning.

6. Research on underlining while studying shows that

   a. many students fail to use it effectively by underlining too much.
   b. limiting the amount of underlining that students can do hinders learning.
   c. both controlled and uncontrolled underlining enhance learning.
   d. underlining in a vivid color such as orange is more effective than using a dull color such as gray.

7. Note-taking appears to be most helpful when

   a. it involves mental processing such as in paraphrasing what the teacher says.
   b. instructors provide students with a complete, detailed outline of the lecture.
   c. it is combined with underlining.
   d. the material involves mostly facts and objective content.

8. Which of the following appears to be the typical effect on learning of cooperative scripts?

   a. The student who listens gains more on the section summarized than the one who summarizes.
   b. The student who summarizes gains more on the section summarized than the one who listens.
   c. Both students gain about the same on the section summarized.
   d. Neither student seems to benefit, but their motivation is generally increased.

9. What do Thomas and Rohwer mean by personal efficacy in their discussions of effective strategies?

   a. The strategy is appropriate to the learning objective.
   b. Students have organized and efficient work habits.
   c. Students engage in a high level of mental processing.
   d. Students feel that a good effort will produce success.

10. The correct order of steps in the SQ4R method is survey, question,

   a. reflect, read, review, and recite.
   b. recite, review, read, and reflect.
   c. read, review, recite, and reflect.
   d. read, reflect, recite, and review.

11. In the study method called "cooperative scripts" the

   a. recaller summarizes while looking at the passage.
   b. high-achieving student is usually designated as the recaller.
   c. listener provides feedback on the accuracy of the summary.
   d. desired group size is from 3-5 individuals.

12. Which of the following is true regarding reciprocal teaching?

   a. It is a method of helping students to develop analytical teaching skills.
   b. Participants work in a reading group in which they alternate playing the role of teacher.
   c. It usually takes the form of a one-to-one tutorial between an older student and a younger one.
   d. It involves two teachers combining their classes so that each can concentrate on separate ability groups.

13. The Instructional Enrichment program seems most successful to date at improving

   a. math achievement.
   b. motivation.
   c. socialization.
   d. scores on IQ tests.

14. An effective way of teaching concepts is to

   a. start with more difficult examples, then decrease the difficulty over time.
   b. select mostly similar examples to illustrate the concept.
   c. start with a rule, present examples, then reintroduce the rule.
   d. all of the above.

15. Which of the following best illustrates the state of functional fixedness?

   a. A student who is used to making "d's" look like "b's" continues to make this error.
   b. A third-grade teacher sees the second-grade achievement scores for her new class, and begins to form expectancies about individuals' abilities.
   c. A student who is trying to solve a math problem explores many different strategies until he gets a reasonable answer.
   d. A student who is using a ruler for drawing lines fails to realize that he can use its metal edge as a scraper to remove paint from his desk.

16. A strategy that would NOT be recommended to enhance group creative problem solving is to

    a. carefully think out a possible solution before suggesting it to others.
    b. establish an informal and relaxed environment.
    c. analyze and juxtapose different problem elements.
    d. think through several solutions before trying a course of action.

17. A major disadvantage of discovery learning is

    a. increased instructional time.
    b. poor retention.
    c. conceptual learning is sacrificed.
    d. all of the above.

18. Which of the following is the clearest illustration of expository teaching?

    a. The social studies teacher organizes students into groups to construct maps of different local towns.
    b. The science teacher positions the entire class in a circle to discuss key issues related to disarmament.
    c. The history teacher asks a question, selects a student to answer, gives feedback, and repeats the process for the next question.
    d. The social studies teacher presents an organized lecture on the structure of United States government.

19. Which of the following is NOT consistent with Ausubel's conception of expository teaching?

    a. Active reception learning
    b. Presentation of advance organizer
    c. Progression from specific to general
    d. Deductive teaching approach

20. The proper order of the initial events of learning in Gagne's sequence is "motivation" followed by

    a. acquisition, apprehending, recall, and retention.
    b. apprehending, retention, recall, and acquisition.
    c. apprehending, acquisition, retention, and recall.
    d. acquisition, retention, recall, and apprehending.

APPLICATION: Schema Experiment

Test several different people on recalling each of the following lists of words. First, have them study the selected list for one minute with the expectancy of later being tested for recall. Second, have them count backwards by three's starting at 21 to eliminate short-term memory of the last few words. Third, give them one minute to write down as many of the words as they can recall.

Compare the average total number of correct responses for each list. Which list would you predict to be recalled more easily? Why? How do actual results compare with your predictions?

List A	List B
Lettuce	Hamburger
Tomato	Lettuce
Cucumber	Cake
Onion	Milk
Steak	Lamb
Lamb	Donuts
Pork	Tomato
Hamburger	Cheese
Milk	Cucumber
Eggs	Bread
Yogurt	Yogurt
Cheese	Onion
Bread	Rolls
Rolls	Pork
Donuts	Eggs
Cake	Steak

APPLICATION: Discovery vs. Reception Learning

Because of your reputation as a nature lover, you are invited by a friend who is a third-grade teacher to present a unit on different types of leaves. Your friend is so excited by the prospect of your guest appearance that she gives you total freedom to structure the content of the presentation as you desire. She recommends, however, that you may want to use either a discovery teaching approach or a conventional lecture approach. You are honored by the invitation and accept.

Regardless of your expertise on leaves (appropriate reference books are available), you feel that you can handle the content. The problem is how to present the lesson, "discovery" or "lecture." Discuss your thoughts on this issue in reference to the following:

A. What planning and teaching procedures would be involved with each method?
B. What advantages and disadvantages would each method offer in planning and implementation?
C. What types of learning outcomes might be engendered by each

approach. Would the most prevalent outcomes differ for the two approaches?

D. Which method would you ultimately choose? Why?

APPLICATION: Study Strategies

The SQ3R and SQ4R systems have a long history and a favorable reputation for helping students to learn instructional material. This exercise is designed to provide some firsthand experiences in using these methods (we'll select SQ4R). Examine your educational psychology course outline and see what chapter you are assigned to read next. Read the description of SQ4R in your text and, if desired, take some notes to remind you of the steps. Then identify an approximately 10-page section in your new chapter. Read and study the chapter applying the SQ4R steps. When you are done, reflect on your experience by evaluating the ease and perceived helpfulness of using each of these steps:

1. Survey
2. Question
3. Read
4. Reflect
5. Recite
6. Review

Did SQ4R, overall, seem helpful? Would it, in your opinion, be worthwhile to teach to a class of students to help them study in a class that you teach?

APPLICATION: Theories into Practice

The statements below refer to practices explicitly supported by the theories of Bruner, Ausubel, or Gagne. Read the statement and identify the source using the first letter of the theorist's name (B, A, or G).

1. Arouse interest in content as the first step to teaching.
2. Use a deductive teaching approach.
3. Advance organizers should be used to introduce lessons.
4. Learning should be flexible and exploratory.
5. Direct students' attention to relevant information.
6. Instructional events must be geared to critical events of learning.
7. Learning is doing.
8. Proceed from the general to the specific.
9. Use direct experiences as the basis for knowledge and acquisition.
10. Activate students' relevant background knowledge as much as possible in teaching a lesson.

COMPUTER EXERCISE

The FREE RECALL program on the EDUCATIONAL PSYCHOLOGY COMPUTER DISK supplement was referred to in the "applications" section for Chapter 5. For this exercise, rerun the program and address the following using your own data or data collected from others.

1. Which of the three lists (nonsense, abstract, or concrete) is associated with the highest degree of recall? Which is associated with the least? Explain the results from the perspective of <u>schema theory.</u>
2. Examine the sequence of words recalled from the <u>concrete</u> list. Do the words seem to be recalled in random order, in the order they were presented, or according to same pattern? Interpret the results with regard to the principles of learning discussed in Chapter 6.

ESSAY/DISCUSSION

1. An uninformed appraisal of types of classroom learning might characterize rote learning as "bad" and meaningful learning as "good." Do you agree? Discuss your perceptions of the rationales and needs for the two types of learning. Why do you think that rote learning is often characterized so negatively by students?

2. Summarize the rationale and procedures for the Reciprocal Teaching method. Then discuss and defend your own views regarding its practicality and likely effectiveness for classroom use.

3. Discuss procedures that you would use to improve students' skills at solving problems.

4. Debates on the relative merits of discovery vs. reception learning generally lead to the conclusion that neither method is "better"; each is advantageous in certain situations. Present your thoughts on this issue by discussing how the following factors might influence your choice between using a discovery or a reception learning approach: (a) student age, (b) type of subject matter (e.g., math vs. English, etc.), and (c) the amount of time available to teach the unit.

ANSWERS

Matching Warm-ups

Quiz 1	Quiz 2
a. 2 (194)	a. 3 (186)
b. 5 (194)	b. 10 (158)
c. 6 (194)	c. 1 (161)
d. 7 (194)	d. 2 (189)
e. 8 (194)	e. 9 (176)
f. 3 (194)	f. 6 (167)
g. 1 (195)	g. 4 (194)
h. 4 (195)	h. 1 (192)
	i. 7 (170)
	j. 5 (165)
	k. 8 (173)
	l. 4 (194)

Key Concepts

1.	C (158)	12.	T (192)
2.	J (170)	13.	S (192)
3.	B (157)	14.	V (193)
4.	G (167)	15.	H (168)
5.	D (161)	16.	Q (186)
6.	P (189)	17.	M (177)
7.	A (157)	18.	N (182)
8.	L (176)	19.	R (189)
9.	K (173)	20.	F (166)
10.	I (170)	21.	E (165)
11.	U (192)	22.	O (183)

Completion Questions

1. rote; meaningful (157)
2. inert (158)
3. schema (159)
4. advance organizers (161)
5. mathemagenic (165)
6. paraphrased (165)
7. cooperative scripts (168)
8. question; reflect; review (170)
9. reciprocal (173)
10. Instructional Enrichment (176)
11. mood; recall; elaborate (171)
12. concepts (177)
13. transfer or learning (181)
14. means-ends (184)
15. functional fixedness (186)
16. discovery (189)
17. expository (192)
18. progressive differentiation (192)
19. deductive (193)
20. motivation (194)

Multiple-Choice

1.	d (157)	11.	c (171)
2.	d (159)	12.	b (173-174)
3.	b (161)	13.	d (176)
4.	d (165)	14.	c (178)
5.	c (165)	15.	d (186)
6.	a (167)	16.	a (186-187)
7.	a (167)	17.	a (190)
8.	b (168)	18.	d (192)
9.	d (169)	19.	c (192)
10.	d (170)	20.	c (194)

Application: Theories into Practices

1.	G (194)	6.	G (194-195)
2.	A (193)	7.	B (190)
3.	A (161)	8.	A (193)
4.	B (189)	9.	B (189-190)
5.	G (194)	10.	A (192-193)

7 Organizing for Instruction

CHAPTER OUTLINE

I. What to Teach and How to Teach It

II. Instructional Objectives
   A. Types of objectives
      1. Must be adapted to the subject matter being taught
      2. Writing clear objectives
   B. Objectives and assessment
      1. Assessments and objectives must be clearly linked
      2. Assessments are samples of student knowledge
      3. Linking test questions to objectives
   C. Bloom's Taxonomy of educational objectives
      1. Types of objectives
      2. Is too much knowledge a dangerous thing?
      3. Behavior content matrices
   D. Research on instructional objectives
   E. Outcomes of learning
      1. Verbal information
      2. Intellectual skill
      3. Cognitive strategy
      4. Attitude
      5. Motor skill
   F. Taxonomy of affective objectives
   G. Psychomotor objectives
   H. Theory into Practice: Planning courses, units, and lessons
      1. Unit objectives and unit tests
      2. Lesson plans and lesson assessments
   I. Teachers on teaching: Instructional objectives
   J. Task analyses

1. Identify prerequisite skills
2. Identify component skills
3. Plan how component skills will be assembled into the final skill

III. Arranging the Classroom for Effective Instruction
  A. Principles of room arrangement
  B. Teachers on teaching: Physical arrangement of the classroom

IV. Models of Effective Instruction
  A. Effective instruction: Not just good teaching
  B. Carroll's model of school learning
  C. The QAIT model of effective instruction
    1. Quality of instruction
    2. Appropriate levels of instruction
    3. Incentive
    4. Time

Summary/Study Questions/Suggested Readings

OBJECTIVES

1. Write both general and specific instructional goals.
2. Set goals that relate to teaching information and cognitive skills, attitudes and values, and physical skills.
3. Break down a complex skill into subskills.
4. Write test questions linked to your instructional goals.
5. List and describe the four alterable aspects of instruction included in the QAIT model.
6. Arrange the desks and other classroom furniture in ways that minimize disturbances and disruptions.

MATCHING WARM-UPS

Match the numbers of the descriptions on the right to the corresponding items on the left. A given item from the right column may be used more than once or not al all.

Quiz 1: Bloom's Taxonomy

_____ a. Synthesis	1.	translating
_____ b. Evaluation	2.	judging against a standard
_____ c. Knowledge	3.	solving novel problems
_____ d. Analysis	4.	creating something
_____ e. Comprehension	5.	recalling information
_____ f. Application	6.	breaking whole into parts

Quiz 2: Gagne's Outcomes of Learning

_____ a. Intellectual skill	1.	feelings about learning
_____ b. Cognitive strategy	2.	factual knowledge
_____ c. Motor skill	3.	problem-solving approach
_____ d. Verbal information	4.	"knowing how"
_____ e. Attitude	5.	physical skills

Quiz 3: Carroll's Model of School Learning

_____ a. Ability to understand instruction	1.	motivation to learn
	2.	effectiveness of lesson
_____ b. Perseverance	3.	general ability to learn
_____ c. Opportunity	4.	amount of learning time
_____ d. Quality of instruction	5.	readiness to learn
_____ e. Aptitude		

Quiz 4: Notable Names

_____ a. Word magic	1.	Bloom
_____ b. Model of school learning	2.	Slavin
_____ c. Task analysis	3.	Mager
_____ d. QAIT	4.	Gagne
_____ e. Behavioral objectives	5.	Bruner
_____ f. Outcomes of learning	6.	Dyer
_____ g. Taxonomy of objectives	7.	Carroll

KEY TERMS

Fill in the blanks below with the letter identifying the following concepts. Each concept is used one time only.

A. Instructional objectives
B. Word magic
C. Assessment
D. Taxonomy of educational objectives
E. Behavior content matrix
F. Affective objectives
G. Psychomotor objectives
H. Backward planning process
I. Task analysis
J. QAIT model

1. The term _____ is used to describe objectives that are fuzzy, vague, and not useful for assessment.

2. The process of breaking objectives down into simpler components is _____.

3. Statements defining what students should master in a given course are called _____.

4. Objectives concerned with attitudes and values are called _____.

5. A chart that shows the cognitive levels of various instructional objectives is called a(n) _____.

6. In Bloom's _____, general types of learning outcomes are classified from simple to complex.

7. _____ is any measure of the degree to which students have learned prescribed instructional objectives.

8. Aspects of instruction that teachers can control form components of the _____.

9. Using a(n) _____ involves first setting long-range goals, then setting unit objectives, and finally planning daily lessons.

10. Objectives concerned with physical skills that students must master are called _____.

COMPLETION QUESTIONS

1. According to Dyer, "fuzzy objectives" use _____ to describe desired performances.

2. Instructional objectives, written as Mager recommends, should specify _____, _____, and _____.

3. Objectives need to be closely linked to _____ for measuring the degree to which they are achieved.

4. In Bloom's taxonomy of objectives, the ordering of learning tasks is knowledge, _____, application, _____, synthesis, and _____.

5. When students recall names and dates, the type of learning in Bloom's taxonomy being demonstrated is _____.

6. When students examine an unfamiliar map and discuss what it shows about the location of cities and the roads that connect them, they are demonstrating the type of learning called _____.

7. A chart classifying lesson objectives according to cognitive level is called a _____.

8. In Gagne's model, _____ consist of procedures students use to solve problems.

9. In Gagne's model, _____ is similar to the knowledge component in Bloom's taxonomy.

10. The attitudes and values that students acquire are stated in _____ objectives.

11. Desired physical behaviors are specified in _____ objectives.

12. A teacher using a _____ process first designs course objectives, then unit objectives, and finally daily lessons.

13. In task analysis, the first step is to identify _____ skills; then _____ skills need to be identified.

14. According to Carroll, _____ is the amount of time allowed for learning.

15. In Carroll's model, _____ is high if students learn material as rapidly as their abilities and levels of prior knowledge allow.

16. The four components of the QAIT model are ____ of instruction, ____ levels of instruction, _____, and _____.

17. The number of elements in the QAIT model that represent alterable elements is _____.

18. The number of elements in the QAIT model that must be adequate for instruction to be effective is _____.

MULTIPLE-CHOICE

Select the best answer for each of the following items.

1. Which of the following verbs would be least desirable for use in a behavioral objective?

   a. Appreciates
   b. Lists
   c. Builds
   d. Isolates

2. Which of the following objectives is complete according to Mager's guidelines?

   a. Using a calculator, the student will solve addition problems correctly.
   b. The student will correctly recall the major bones of the human body when asked to.
   c. Without using notes, the student will correctly identify the functions of four major organs in the digestive system.
   d. Given colored pictures of fruits and vegetables, the student will correctly classify each type with a high degree of accuracy.

3. The term "word magic" is used to refer to objectives that

   a. are not specific enough to be meaningful.
   b. are very carefully phrased so that their meaning is exact and unambiguous.
   c. use the least number of words possible while still conveying the proper meaning.
   d. deal with behaviors in the affective domain.

4. An objective states that students should be able to identify 90% of the over 100 chemistry elements when shown their symbols (Na=sodium) from the periodic table. An appropriate assessment would, in most cases, test students on

   a. a random sample of elements (say 10-20).
   b. all elements.
   c. 90% of the elements.
   d. the most difficult 10% of the elements.

5. Bloom's taxonomy orders different types of objectives on the basis of

   a. importance.
   b. alphabetical position.
   c. frequency of use.
   d. complexity.

6. A student has just completed a computer programming course. Which of the following learning outcomes would be classified as synthesis in Bloom's taxonomy?

   a. Discussing the value of programming to society
   b. Writing an original program
   c. Identifying the meaning of different programming commands
   d. Interpreting how an existing program operates

7. The highest or most complex type of learning in Bloom's taxonomy is

   a. evaluation.
   b. analysis.
   c. synthesis.
   d. application.

8. A student presents her views on the desirability of having the current president nominate Supreme Court Justices. The type of learning illustrated is

   a. evaluation.
   b. understanding.
   c. application.
   d. synthesis.

9. Research on behavioral objectives has shown

a. clearly positive results favoring the use of instructional objectives.
b. clearly negative results suggesting that objectives not be used.
c. mixed results that sometimes favor using objectives and sometimes do not.
d. inconclusive findings since usage of objectives cannot be manipulated experimentally.

10. A behavior content matrix is designed to help teachers

a. plan how a particular skill will be taught.
b. plan how a particular skill will be assessed.
c. increase the use of high level objectives.
d. all of the above.

11. As defined in Gagne's model, an example of an intellectual skill would be

a. knowing how to convert a Celsius temperature reading to Fahrenheit.
b. recalling the number of letters in the alphabet.
c. developing a strategy to defeat a new opponent in chess.
d. all of the above.

12. A student discriminates between the forms for representing French feminine and masculine nouns. In Gagne's model, this type of learning represents

a. a cognitive strategy.
b. verbal information.
c. an affective skill.
d. an intellectual skill.

13. A student recites the names of all members of the New York Yankees baseball team. In Gagne's model this type of learning represents

a. a cognitive strategy.
b. verbal information.
c. an affective skill.
d. an intellectual skill.

14. In contrast to Bloom's taxonomy of cognitive objectives, Krathwohl's taxonomy of affective objectives

a. has played a relatively limited role in schools.
b. has produced consistently positive research results.
c. allows for clear separation between elements.
d. permits fairly easy, unambiguous classification of student behaviors.

15. In using a <u>backwards</u> planning process, a teacher should first

a. plan the daily lessons that students will receive.
b. construct the end-of-course examination.
c. establish objectives for the whole course.
d. identify the first unit and establish objectives for it.

16. After identifying prerequisite skills in a task analysis, the next step is to

a. plan how the prerequisite skills will be assembled into the final skill.
b. identify component skills.
c. identify how those prerequisite skills can be taught.
d. classify task objectives according to the type of learning they involve.

17. Which of the following procedures for room arrangement is <u>not</u> recommended?

a. Keep students' desks away from doorways to prevent blockage of traffic.
b. Arrange student desks so that all can be seen from the teacher's desk.
c. Keep frequently used supplies, such as paper, in a restricted area to discourage wasteful usage.
d. Keep students as close as possible to instructional presentations to increase level of participation.

18. In Carroll's model, ability to understand instruction is most directly influenced by

a. the amount of time students are willing to actively spend on a task.
b. the amount of time available for learning.
c. students' general abilities to learn.
d. students' readiness to learn a particular lesson.

19. Relative to Carroll's model, the QAIT model described by Slavin is

a. virtually identical, but uses different names for similar elements.
b. very different in its interpretation of important elements of school learning.
c. similar, but includes only the unalterable elements of Carroll's model.
d. similar, but includes only the alterable elements of Carroll's model.

20. Which of the following alternatives pairs an element from Carroll's model with an element having the same meaning from the QAIT model?

a. Perseverance: Time
b. Opportunity: Quality of instruction
c. Aptitude: Incentive
d. Perseverance: Incentive

APPLICATION: Instructional Objectives

Listed below are "attempted" behavioral instructive objectives for different subjects. Each is flawed in some critical way. Identify the error and indicate the type of change required.

A. The student will understand the procedures for dissecting the following animals: frog, fish, and hamster.

B. Given an electric drill, power circular saw, screwdriver, 4 ft. x 4 ft. sheet of plywood, and other requested tools and hardware (sandpaper, screws, etc.), the student will build a birdhouse.

C. Using the textbook and class notes, the student will learn the meaning of at least 8 out of 10 chemical equations.

D. The student will identify 15 different birds in the field.

E. Each football lineman will run one-mile in 9 minutes or less.

F. The student will pass 5 out of 6 math quizzes during the term.

G. Students will appreciate the clarity and simplicity of Hemingway's style.

APPLICATION: Taxonomy of Educational Objectives

In Chapter 3 on behavioral theories of learning, you were introduced to Pavlov's model of classical conditioning. In review, it involved discovering that the presentation of the unconditioned stimulus (UCS), meat, to a hungry dog elicited the unconditioned response (UCR), salivating. When the neutral stimulus, bell, was presented, no salivating occurred. During training, the bell was rung just before the meat was presented. After training, ringing the bell, which then served as a conditioned stimulus (CS) produced the conditioned response (CR), salivating.

Listed below are a number of different learning tasks someone who has studied classical condition might perform. Classify each using the following 6 elements from Bloom's taxonomy.

1. Knowledge	4. Analysis
2. Comprehensive	5. Synthesis
3. Application	6. Application

A. A student uses the classical conditioning model to condition her dog to bark when the doorbell rings.

B. A student discusses the ethics of using classical conditioning and other behavioral principles with human beings in school settings.

C. A student defines the meaning UCS, CS, UCR, and CR in his own words.

D. In experimenting with classical conditioning principles in the laboratory, a student self-discovers the principles of extinction and generalization.

E. A student compares the components of classical conditioning with those of Skinner's operant conditioning model.

F. A student identifies the UCS, CS, UCR, and CR in Pavlov's experiment.

APPLICATION: Task Analysis

Use the three-step process proposed by Gagne to analyze one (or more) of the following tasks:

1. Starting a car
2. Baking a cake
3. Drawing squares of different sizes
4. Solving an equation of the form: $X + 1 = 5$
5. Changing a tire
6. Labeling the states on a map of the United States

APPLICATION: Field Experience on Classroom Environments

Observe two or three different classrooms at the grade levels in which you plan to teach. Evaluate each with regard to the following four principles of room arrangements described in your textbook:

A. Keep high traffic areas free of congestion.
B. Be sure that students can easily be seen by the teacher.
C. Keep frequently used teaching materials and student supplies readily accessible.
D. Be certain students can see instructional presentations and displays.

Do the teachers observed seem to differ in their application of these principles? If so, are any implications evident for classroom discipline, disturbances, and the effectiveness of instruction in general?

APPLICATION: Computer Exercise

The EDUCATIONAL PSYCHOLOGY COMPUTER DISK for your textbook contains a program called "OBJECTIVES." It describes the experiences of "Mrs. Counts" in trying to write an acceptable instructional objective for a unit in her social studies course. In interacting with the program, you will be asked to evaluate Mrs. Counts' decisions. You will receive feedback on the appropriateness of those responses and then be given an opportunity to test your knowledge of instructional objectives on a quiz. If you have access to the program, be sure to give it a try.

ESSAY/DISCUSSION

1. Identify the four components of the QAIT model. What attributes do they have in common and how do they differ? Conclude your discussion by identifying a learning experience you have recently had (such as in one of your college courses) and evaluating how successfully your instructor handled each component.

2. Are instructional objectives really needed or are they just something textbooks and teaching manuals recommend? Present your views on this issue, after first describing the different forms instructional objectives commonly take and the functions they are designed to achieve.

3. A teacher writes an instructional objective for his history course as follows:

   > Students will understand the implications of the Battle of Gettysburg for subsequent developments in the Civil War.

   His principal objects to this objective, arguing that it lacks performance conditions, an action verb, and an evaluation criterion. The teacher argues that it captures exactly what he is trying to accomplish and that rephrasing it in specific behavioral terms would make it seem trivial. The principal (of course) emerges victorious in this battle, but deep down the teacher remains unconvinced.

   What is your view regarding this issue? Would you side with the principal or the instructor? Are specific behavioral objectives necessary or can "general" ones like the teacher's be useful? Explain.

4. Describe the purposes and specific components of Bloom's taxonomy of educational objectives. In your opinion, can learning tasks be validly classified into those categories? Explain.

5. Describe, using a familiar teaching area as an example, how a backward planning process would be applied.

6. A new teacher is in the process of arranging her classroom and asks you for advice on where to put desks, supplies, etc. Discuss some suggestions you might provide to help her minimize disturbances and disruptions.

ANSWERS

Matching Warm-Ups

Quiz 1	Quiz 2	Quiz 3	Quiz 4
a. 4 (207)	a. 4 (211)	a. 5 (221)	a. 6 (204)
b. 2 (207)	b. 3 (211)	b. 1 (221)	b. 7 (221)
c. 5 (207)	c. 5 (211)	c. 4 (221)	c. 4 (217)
d. 6 (207)	d. 2 (211)	d. 2 (221)	d. 2 (222)
e. 1 (207)	e. 1 (211)	e. 3 (221)	e. 3 (202)
f. 3 (207)			f. 4 (210)
			g. 1 (206)

Key Terms

1. B (204)
2. I (217)
3. A (201)
4. F (211)
5. E (208)
6. D (206)
7. C (204)
8. J (222)
9. H (214)
10. G (212)

Completion Questions

1. word magic (204)
2. performance, conditions, criteria (202-203)
3. assessment (204)
4. comprehension, analysis, evaluation (207)
5. knowledge (207)
6. analysis (207)
7. behavior content matrix (208)
8. cognitive strategies (211)
9. verbal information (211)
10. affective (211)
11. psychomotor (212)
12. backward planning (214)
13. prerequisite; component (217)
14. opportunity (221)
15. quality of instruction (221)
16. quality; appropriate; incentive; time (222)
17. four (222)
18. four (222)

Multiple-Choice

1. a (204)
2. c (202-203)
3. a (204)
4. a (205)
5. d (206)
6. b (207)
7. a (207)
8. a (207)
9. c (209)
10. d (208)
11. a (210)
12. d (210)
13. b (210)
14. a (212)
15. c (214)
16. b (217)
17. c (218)
18. d (221)
19. d (221-222)
20. d (221-222)

Application: Writing Instructional Objectives

A. No clear performance, conditions, or criterion
B. No criterion
C. No clear performance
D. No conditions (e.g., can she use binoculars?; how much time is available?)
E. No conditions (on track? on field?)
F. No clear performance (what is "pass?"); no conditions
G. No clear performance, conditions, or criterion

Application: Taxonomy of Educational Objectives

A. Application
B. Evaluation
C. Comprehension
D. Synthesis
E. Analysis
F. Knowledge

8 The Lesson

CHAPTER OUTLINE

I. Parts of the Lesson
   A. Overview of seven components
   B. Sample lessons

II. Lessons: Step-by-Step
   A. State instructional objectives and orient students to learn
   B. Review prerequisites
   C. Present new material
      1. Organization
      2. Explanations
      3. Demonstrations
      4. Maintaining attention
   D. Conduct learning probes
      1. Questions
      2. How to ask questions
   E. Provide independent practice
      1. Do not assign independent practice until you are sure students can do it
      2. Keep independent practice assignments short
      3. Give clear instructions
      4. Get students started, and then avoid interruptions
      5. Monitor independent work
      6. Collect independent work and include it in student grades
   F. Assess performance and provide feedback
   G. Provide distributed practice and review
   H. Teachers on teaching: Lessons and homework

III. Direct Instruction
   A. Theory into practice: Direct instructional methods
      1. Madeline Hunter's mastery teaching
      2. Missouri Mathematics Program
      3. DISTAR
      4. Similarities among direct instruction methods
   B. Research on direct instruction methods
      1. "Master Teacher" strategies
      2. "Systematic Instruction" models
      3. Direct instruction: Conclusions

IV. Discussions
   A. Whole-class discussions
      1. Examples
      2. Information before discussion
   B. Small-group discussions
   C. Teachers on teaching: Class discussions

V. Humanistic Education
   A. Open schools
      1. What they are
      2. Research on open education
   B. Humanistic education vs. direct instruction

Summary/Study Questions/Suggested Readings

CHAPTER OBJECTIVES

1. List the steps that are considered fundamental to effective lesson presentation.
2. Use various types of learning probes to monitor student comprehension.
3. Present and monitor independent practice assignments that help students learn.
4. List three widely used forms of direct instruction and describe situations in which each can be used.
5. Employ class discussions in appropriate situations.
6. Understand the goals of humanistic education.

MATCHING WARM-UPS

Match the numbers of the descriptions on the right to the corresponding items on the left. A given item from the right column may be used more than once or not at all.

Quiz 1: Direct Instruction Methods

_____ a. Madeline Hunter's Mastery Teaching
_____ b. MMP
_____ c. Slavin's Model
_____ d. DISTAR

1. Directed toward teaching math
2. 7 steps ending with distributed practice
3. A general guide for teaching in any area
4. Used exclusively for teaching Spanish
5. A very specific, structured approach

Quiz 2: Notable Names

_____ a. Humanistic psychology
_____ b. Progressive education
_____ c. Mastery teaching model
_____ d. Direct instruction
_____ e. Summerhill

1. A. S. Neil
2. M. Hunter
3. R. Gagne
4. B. Rosenshine
5. J. Dewey
6. C. Rogers

KEY TERMS

Fill in the blanks below with the letters identifying the following concepts. Each concept is used one time only.

A. Mental Set
B. Learning probes
C. Wait time
D. Choral response
E. Independent practice
F. Seatwork
G. Direct instruction
H. Process-product studies
I. Madeline Hunter's Mastery Teaching Program
J. Missouri Mathematics Program
K. DISTAR model
L. Grade equivalents
M. Inquiry training
N. Humanistic education
O. Open schools
P. Learning stations

1. A direct instruction model that uses highly structured materials to teach reading and math is the _____.

2. When an entire class answers in unison, the students are making a(n) _____.

3. A teaching approach designed to increase students' skills at asking questions while problem-solving is _____.

4. Measures of achievement expressed as the expected norms for specific grade levels are _____.

5. Work that students do on their own in class or somewhere else represents _____; work done exclusively in class, however, is called _____.

6. Asking students to make brief responses during a lesson represents use of _____.

7. An attitude or expectancy for learning is called a(n) _____.

8. A direct instruction model consisting of the steps of anticipatory set, input and modeling, checking understanding, guided practice, and independent practice is the _____.

9. Areas where students work on independent projects are _____.

10. A general term for highly structured, focused, and teacher-controlled methods of teaching is _____.

11. A direct instruction model geared to the teaching of mathematics is the _____.

12. The affective aspects of school, creative learning, and maximizing one's potential are emphasized by the _____ movement.

13. Contrasts between the methods used by effective and ineffective teachers are made in _____.

14. Programs designed to promote the values of humanistic education are called _____.

15. The interval that a teacher allows a student to answer a question before calling on another student is called _____.

COMPLETION QUESTIONS

1. The model presented in your textbook begins a lesson by stating _____ and by _____ students to the material.

2. Questioning techniques that give students practice and teachers feedback are called _____.

3. After a lesson is presented in class, homework should be assigned to provide _____ practice.

4. The interval a teacher allows a student to take in answering a question is _____.

5. Asking a question for the entire class to answer is intended to elicit _____ responding.

6. Teachers assign _____ to engage students in independent practice in class.

7. Direct instruction is derived from _____ studies in which the teaching practices of successful teachers have been recorded.

8. An initial step in Madeline Hunter's Mastery Teaching Program is creating an _____ set.

9. Unlike some other direct instruction programs, the _____ program uses a specific set of materials and procedures for teaching math and reading.

10. The most thoroughly evaluated of the "master teacher" direct instruction strategies is the _____.

11. Scores based on expected performance levels at specific grade levels are _____.

12. The two forms of class discussions are _____ and _____.

13. In _____ training, students are presented with a puzzling event and must ask questions and try out theories to explain what happened.

14. _____ educators often prefer written evaluations to letter grades, standardized testing, and other formal evaluation methods.

15. A book that describes a student-centered learning approach used in England is _____.

MULTIPLE-CHOICE

Select the best answer for each of the following items.

1. Which one of the following practices is recommended in presenting a lesson?

   a. Maintaining a serious attitude with only occasional use of humor
   b. Highlighting important points with remarks such as "It is particularly important to note that..."
   c. Starting class a few minutes after the period begins to give students a chance to settle down
   d. All of the above

2. Which of the following shows the correct sequence of three recommended components of teaching a lesson?

   a. Review prerequisites, present new material, orient students
   b. Provide distributed practice, present new material, review prerequisites
   c. Orient students, provide independent practice, present lesson
   d. Review prerequisites, present new material, and conduct probes

3. The clearest example of a learning probe, as defined in the textbook, is a(n)

   a. homework assignment.
   b. examination.
   c. question to the class.
   d. report card grade.

4. Research on questioning suggests that

   a. factual questions should primarily be used with secondary school students.
   b. teachers tend to use shorter wait times with low achievers.
   c. frequency of questioning is unrelated to student achievement
   d. thought-provoking questions become increasingly less effective in higher grades.

5. The questioning strategy favored by your textbook is to

   a. pose the question first and then call on students in a prescribed way.
   b. call on a student at random and then pose the question.
   c. pose the question to the class and then call on a student at random.
   d. pose the question first and call on high-achievers if the question is difficult or low-achievers if it is easy.

6. In a study by Tobin (1986), an appropriate wait time following a question was _____ second(s).

   a. 1
   b. 3
   c. 15
   d. 25

7. Choral responding seems most appropriate when

   a. classes are very small.
   b. students are relatively young (elementary school age).
   c. content is high in difficulty.
   d. there is only one correct answer.

8. The general conclusion from research on seatwork is that it is

   a. overused and misused.
   b. highly effective for poorly motivated students.
   c. more effective for the typical student than receiving instruction directly from the teacher.
   d. underused with low-achievers.

9. Independent practice assignments should be made fairly

   a. long.
   b. short.
   c. difficult.
   d. behavioral.

10. Which of the following should teachers <u>not</u> do in providing independent practice?

   a. Circulate among the students to see how they are doing
   b. Give intermittent explanations to the entire class to provide stopping points
   c. Monitor the work of individual students
   d. Collect students' work and grade it

11. Which of the following modifiers is inconsistent with the goals of direct instruction?

   a. Discovery oriented
   b. Academically focused
   c. Sequenced
   d. Structured

12. The focus of process-product studies is

   a. recording the teaching practices of good teachers.
   b. testing selected methods with randomly selected teachers
   c. identifying the teaching methods that students feel are most desirable.
   d. categorizing the methods that principals require their teachers to use.

13. DISTAR can be described as a

   a. discovery-oriented teaching approach.
   b. direct instruction approach that offers guidelines to enhance teaching of mathematics.
   c. direct instruction approach depending upon specific materials and procedures.
   d. humanistic teaching approach.

14. Research on direct instruction models has shown that

   a. "master teacher" strategies are more effective than "systematic instruction" strategies.
   b. highly systematic forms are very effective in increasing basic skills.
   c. Madeline Hunter's model appears to produce the most consistent positive outcomes.
   d. such models are generally ineffective in raising achievement.

15. The discussion method of teaching would be least desirable when

   a. questions in a subject contain complex answers.
   b. questions in a subject contain several answers.
   c. subject matter contains clearly definable and masterable objectives.
   d. affective objectives are of particular importance.

16. Small-group discussion differs from whole-group discussion by

   a. having leaders appointed.
   b. requiring less student preparation on the topic.
   c. requiring more direct involvement by the teacher.
   d. all of the above.

17. Humanistic education is philosophically similar to the earlier

   a. behavioristic movement of Skinner.
   b. Gestalt psychology orientation.
   c. progressive education movement of Dewey.
   d. neobehavioristic movement by Osgood.

18. A humanistic educator would be least interested in helping a child to

   a. work independently.
   b. perform better on standardized tests.
   c. value school and education.
   d. develop effective problem-solving strategies.

19. Research evaluations of the amount of learning that occurs in open schools in comparison to traditional schools have generally shown

   a. no differences between the two orientations.
   b. the open schools to be superior.
   c. the traditional schools to be superior.

20. Regarding the relative effectiveness of humanistic education and direct instruction, the interpretation favored in your textbook is

a. humanistic education seems preferable.
b. direct instruction seems preferable.
c. neither method has worked well, making it important for educators to develop new strategies.
d. each method offers important advantages for particular types of objectives.

<u>APPLICATION:</u> Improving Teaching Practices

Consider each of the following teaching episodes and recommend ways in which the instructor's practices can be improved. (Do not be concerned if you are unfamiliar with the subject and the details of the episode; your suggestions are to be only preliminary ones, based on general impressions of what occurred.)

A. At exactly 10:00, when second period should begin, Mr. Pensak walks quickly into his high school biology classroom. He takes out his notes, nods a brief hello to the class, positions himself squarely behind the podium and begins. "Today's topic is the nervous system. Think of the nervous system as long chains of connecting cells, called neurons. Neurons consist of four basic parts..." For the duration of the class he continues in this fashion, providing an informative, well-organized presentation. Interactions with the class are restricted to announcements and reminders, such as "remember to show the synapse on the diagrams that you do for homework." Unfortunately, although Mr. Pensak's material is well-organized, appropriate in difficulty, and presented at a suitable pace, students learn very little. One student's notes start with information that was presented five minutes after the lecture began. Another's notes are mostly doodlings. Quite a few glance frequently at their watches.

B. Ms. Calaway, the junior-high social studies teacher, decides to use the discussion method to teach the philosophy and political practices of communism relative to democracy. The students have just completed a unit on European nations and are about to study Russia and its satellites. She divides the class at random into three groups of six members each. She appoints a leader of each group and gives him/her a list of questions of the type "Can the quality of life be as high under communism as it is under democracy?" She tells the groups to begin discussing their questions. At first many voices are heard, but soon it grows quieter and there is more laughter and less discussion. One group is passing around photographs that one of the students brought. In others, students are mostly thumbing through books or whispering in pairs. While visiting the groups to stimulate discussion, Ms. Calaway is asked by one of the students, "What is communism anyway?"

C. Ms. Bowyer is reviewing French vocabulary words in her introductory course. She starts with the first student, Mary, and says the French word, "garcon." Mary responds with the English equivalent, boy. Ms. Bowyer says "bon," and reads the next word to the student behind Mary. She then proceeds down that row and through the next, calling on the students in seating order, until all have received one chance to respond. Ms. Bowyer feels that the exercise is going well and that students are attentive. In truth, however, close observation would indicate that only those within three or four questions of being called on are interested at all. As a change of pace, Ms. Bowyer calls on Carlton who had already answered an earlier question. Carlton is caught completely by surprise and says, "Ah, could you repeat that word?"

<u>APPLICATION:</u> Field Observation of Lesson Presentations

Identify two or three different classes (college or precollege) which you normally attend or visit as a field activity. Be sure that the classes are ones in which teachers typically present lessons as opposed to laboratory or independent study classes. Observe each teacher present two lessons. Evaluate each presentation relative to the model discussed in your textbook and shown below. Then answer the following questions: (A) Did the presentation include each of the major steps? (B) Did the steps appear to be effectively implemented? (C) If any steps were omitted, did the lesson appear less effective as a result? (D) Which step(s) seemed more or less critical than others in influencing the overall quality of the presentation? (E) Which instructor (or individual presentation) appeared to be most effective? Why?

The model is:

1. State learning objectives and orient students to lesson
2. Review prerequisites
3. Present new material
4. Conduct learning probes
5. Provide independent practice
6. Assess performance and provide feedback
7. Provide distributed practice and review

<u>APPLICATION:</u> Direct Instruction vs. Discussion

For the subject that you plan to teach (English, history, math, foreign language, etc.), identify five different topics (or lessons) that appear best suited for teaching by <u>direct instruction</u> and five others that appear best suited for teaching through <u>discovery.</u> After you construct your lists, explain the rationale for your selections.

ESSAY/DISCUSSION

1. Teaching is alternately described as an "art" (an inborn skill) and a "science." Identify and briefly define the "parts of a lesson" that comprise your textbook's model of effective classroom teaching, and discuss which, if any, seem more "art" and which, if any, seem more "science." Give a rationale for your decisions.

2. Briefly describe and contrast the following direct instruction models: Madeline Hunter's Mastery Teaching Program, the Missouri Mathematics Program, and DISTAR. Based on the general background and evaluations provided in your textbook, which model appeals to you most at this time? Explain.

3. Suppose you are teaching a course in American History to eighth-grade students. For what types of topics (don't worry about specific historical content) might you use the discussion method of teaching instead of lecture-recitation? When using discussion, do you feel that you would tend to favor a small-group or whole-class orientation? Explain your answer.

4. Define "humanistic education" and describe, using examples, how its goals (or values) differ from those emphasized in direct instruction methods.

5. Open education attracted a considerable following during the early 1970s, but its popularity has declined in recent years. What is the main philosophy and orientation of open education? Why, in your opinion, is open education less accepted today as a primary teaching method?

6. You are about to teach a class in a subject area and grade level for which you are trained. Describe different strategies for using learning probes in presenting a lesson to that class and indicate which particular strategy you feel would probably work best.

ANSWERS

Matching Warm-Ups

Quiz 1	Quiz 2
a. 3 (248)	a. 6 (262)
b. 1 (249)	b. 5 (262)
c. 2 (239)	c. 2 (248)
d. 5 (250)	d. 4 (247)
	e. 1 (262)

Key Terms

1.	K (250)	9.	P (266)
2.	D (243)	10.	G (247)
3.	M (257)	11.	J (249)
4.	L (253)	12.	N (262)
5.	E;F (243)	13.	H (248)
6.	B (239)	14.	O (266)
7.	A (234)	15.	C (242)
8.	I (248)		

Completion Questions

1. objectives, orienting (229)
2. learning probes (239)
3. distributed (247)
4. wait time (242)
5. choral (243)
6. seatwork (243)
7. process-product (248)
8. anticipatory (248)
9. DISTAR (250)
10. Missouri Mathematics Program (249)
11. grade equivalents (253)
12. whole-class; small-group (256)
13. inquiry (257)
14. humanistic (262)
15. Summerhill (262)

Multiple-Choice

1.	b (237)	11.	a (247)
2.	d (239)	12.	a (248)
3.	c (239)	13.	c (250)
4.	b (242)	14.	b (254)
5.	c (242)	15.	c (255)
6.	b (242)	16.	a (261)
7.	d (242)	17.	c (262)
8.	a (243)	18.	b (263-264)
9.	b (244)	19.	c (266)
10.	b (244)	20.	d (267)

9 Accommodating Student Differences

CHAPTER OUTLINE

I. The Problem of Student Differences
   A. Types of differences
   B. Learning styles
   C. Providing appropriate levels of instruction

II. Grouping Students by Ability
   A. Ability grouping between classes
      1. Research on between-class ability grouping
      2. Special education and gifted programs
   B. Ability grouping within classes
      1. Research on within-class ability grouping
      2. Applicability of within-class ability grouping
   C. Teachers on teaching: Ability grouping
   D. General principles of ability grouping
   E. Theory into practice: Ability-grouped active teaching
      1. Assigning students to teaching groups
      2. Pacing and testing
      3. Preparing lessons
      4. Seating arrangements
      5. Daily activities
         a. Before class begins
         b. Opening
         c. Teaching group lessons
         d. Seatwork
         e. Quizzes and tests
         f. Grades

III. Effective Use of Reading Groups
   A. Assigning students to groups
      1. Use diagnostic testing
      2. Establish up to three groups
   B. Content and pace of lessons
      1. Take into account special needs of each group
      2. Use frequent assessment
   C. Guidelines for instruction
   D. Cooperative integrated reading and composition

IV. Mastery Learning
   A. Basic principles
      1. Degree of learning = (time spent)/(time needed)
      2. Mastery learning in practice
      3. Research findings
   B. Theory into practice: Mastery learning
      1. Lesson preparation
         a. Formative and summative quizzes
         b. Mastery criteria
         c. Corrective instruction
         d. Enrichment activities
      2. Major activities
         a. Orient students to mastery
         b. Teach the lesson
         c. Give the formative "no-fault" quiz
         d. Give students either corrective instruction or enrichment activities
         e. Give the summative quiz and report the scores to students

V. Individualized Instruction
   A. Programmed instruction
   B. Team Assisted Individualization
   C. Tutoring
      1. Peer tutoring
      2. Research on peer tutoring
      3. Adult tutoring
   D. Teachers on teaching: Tutoring
   E. Informal remediation and enrichment

VI. Computer-Assisted Instruction
   A. History of CAI
      1. Early work
      2. PLATO system
      3. Microcomputer revolution
      4. Software issues
   B. Types of CAI programs
      1. Drill-and-practice programs
      2. Tutorial programs
      3. Simulations
      4. Educational games
      5. Utility programs

C. Research on CAI
   1. Results from research studies
   2. Computer programming

VII. Appropriate Levels of Instruction: Review of General Principles

Summary/Study Questions/Suggested Readings

CHAPTER OBJECTIVES

1. List the types of student differences that are most important to consider when teaching a class.
2. Explain the disadvantages of using tracking--or between-class ability grouping--to accommodate student differences.
3. Plan a class period in which within-class ability grouping is used to teach basic skills to elementary school students.
4. Describe how a unit could be taught using mastery learning.
5. Understand how computers can be used to provide individualized instruction.

MATCHING WARM-UPS

Match the numbers of the descriptions on the right to the corresponding items on the left. A given item from the right column may be used more than once or not at all.

Quiz 1: Learning Styles

_____ a. Field dependence	1. Focus on accuracy
_____ b. Field independence	2. People-oriented
_____ c. Reflectivity	3. Focus on speed
_____ d. Impulsivity	4. Can separate parts from the whole

Quiz 2: Adaptive Methods

_____ a. AGAT	1. Self-pacing, formative quizzes, and correctives
_____ b. Mastery learning	2. Cooperative reading groups
_____ c. Joplin plan	3. Highly structured self-instructional materials
_____ d. CIRC	4. Within-class ability grouping
_____ e. Programmed instruction	5. One-to-one instruction
_____ f. CAI	6. Cooperative learning in mixed ability teams
_____ g. Tutoring	7. Use of the computer for teaching
	8. A regrouping method

Quiz 3: Notable Names

_____ a. Early CAI work		1. Slavin
_____ b. Ability-Grouped Active Teaching		2. Carroll
_____ c. Field independence		3. Atkinson
_____ d. Learning=F(time spent/time needed)		4. Bloom
_____ e. Logo language		5. Witkin
_____ f. College-level individualization		6. Keller
_____ g. Mastery learning		7. Papert
_____ h. Team Assisted Individualization		

KEY TERMS

Fill in the blanks below with the letters identifying the following concepts. Each concept is used one time only.

A. Tracks
B. Learning styles
C. Field dependence
D. Field independence
E. Impulsivity/reflectivity
F. Between-class ability grouping
G. Regrouping
H. Joplin Plan
I. Within-class ability grouping
J. Ability-Grouped Active Teaching
K. Cooperative Integrated Reading and Composition
L. Diagnostic tests
M. Mastery learning
N. Formative quizzes
O. Summative quizzes
P. Mastery criteria
Q. Corrective instruction
R. Enrichment activities
S. Individualized instruction
T. Programmed instruction
U. Team Assisted Individualization
V. Peer tutoring
W. Remediation
X. Computer-assisted instruction
Y. Software
Z. Drill-and-practice programs
AA. Tutorial programs
BB. Linear programs
CC. Branching programs
DD. Simulation programs
EE. Utility programs

1. Students' typical manners of processing information represents their _____.

2. Computer programs that allow students to practice what they have learned and receive immediate feedback are _____.

3. A form of ability grouping in which students attend regular classes for most of the day but same-ability classes for instruction in reading or math is called _____.

4. Final tests of the degree to which content has been mastered are called _____.

5. Individualized instruction delivered by a computer is _____.

6. A learning style that concerns the extent to which individuals focus on accuracy and precision as opposed to speed is _____.

7. A general term for computer programs that provide instruction or perform special functions is _____.

8. A general term for a teaching method that allows students to work by themselves at their own pace is _____.

9. Students who fail to master an objective are given _____ to improve their skills in that area.

10. Highly structured lessons that students complete at their own pace constitute _____.

11. Students who work well in groups but have difficulty separating the parts of stimuli from the whole are characterized as showing _____; those who are skilled at analyzing patterns and do well with problem-solving tasks are characteristized as showing _____.

12. A program in which students work on individualized materials in four-member mixed-ability teams is _____.

13. To determine whether students have achieved test objectives, _____ are set as evaluation standards.

14. The type of ability grouping in which high- and low-achievers work in different groups in the same classroom is _____.

15. The extra help given to students who are having difficulty learning is called _____.

16. A method of teaching mathematics using within-class ability grouping is _____.

17. Computer tutorial programs that vary the content of a lesson based on student responses are called _____.

18. A regrouping method in which students are assigned to mixed-ability reading groups across grade levels is the _____.

19. While completing a lesson, students may be given _____ to determine whether additional instruction is needed.

20. A system that emphasizes the achievement of instructional objectives by all students is _____.

21. Having one student teach another is called _____.

22. The information needed to determine students' assignments to ability groups is usually provided from _____.

23. Computer programs that do not directly teach, but help students perform school tasks are called _____.

24. _____ are computer programs designed to teach new concepts by adapting content and pacing to learner needs.

25. Computer tutorial programs that present materials in a predetermined sequence are called _____.

26. Computer models of real-life problems for students to explore are presented in _____.

27. Students who complete work early may be assigned _____ to extend or broaden their involvement with the subject.

28. Classes or programs designated for students of different ability levels are called _____.

29. The type of ability grouping in which high- and low-achievers are assigned to different classes is _____.

30. A method in which students practice reading by performing different study activities together is _____.

COMPLETION QUESTIONS

1. Joanna works on her assignment extremely slowly, checking each answer over and over again to ensure it is right. She is demonstrating a _____ learning style.

2. Karl has tremendous difficulty doing math word problems because he cannot isolate the critical information from the verbal context. One might characterize his learning style as_____.

3. Students are assigned to different classes on the basis of measured ability in _____ ability grouping.

4. Students in a given class are assigned to different ability groups in _____ ability grouping.

5. Under a regrouping plan, students spend most of the day in a _____ class.

6. The two subjects for which ability grouping is most commonly used are _____ and _____.

7. The optimal number of ability groups to establish in a class appears to be _____ groups.

8. The AGAT method was designed as an ability grouped version of one of the direct instruction programs you studied in the previous chapter. The name of that program is _____.

9. Under Ability-Grouped-Active Teaching, students are assigned _____ in class to practice what they have learned during the lessons.

10. A method designed to involve students in cooperative follow-up activity in reading is _____.

11. In Carroll's model, the degree of school learning is a function of time spent divided by _____.

12. Under a mastery learning approach, instructors attempt to bring all students to mastery by allowing learning _____ to differ.

13. A mastery learning model found to be successful at the college level is the _____.

14. A test used at the end of a course to evaluate how much has been learned is a _____ quiz.

15. Another name for a "no-fault" quiz used to determine instructional needs is a _____ quiz.

16. Under mastery learning, students who fail to reach criterion on a test are given _____ to help them succeed on the next try.

17. Under mastery learning, students who achieve the mastery criterion early are given _____ to broaden their understanding of the subject area.

18. A form of individualized learning in which students complete highly structured self-instructional material at their own pace is _____.

19. Under the _____ model, students complete individualized work in four-member mixed-ability groups.

20. The type of peer tutoring in which an older student teaches a younger student is called _____ tutoring.

21. An early CAI system that linked a central computer to hundreds of terminals, and used speech synthesizers with touch-sensitive screens was _____.

22. Computerized lessons that attempt to teach content as a teacher might do are called _____ programs.

23. _____ programs vary the content presented according to student answers, whereas _____ programs present the same content to all students, regardless of answers or performances.

24. _____ programs model "real-life" problems for students to solve.

25. Word-processing programs and text-editing programs are examples of _____ programs, since they allow the computer to be used as a tool for performing valuable tasks.

26. A computer language designed expressly for young children is _____.

MULTIPLE-CHOICE

Select the best answer for each of the following items.

1. The method known as "tracking" represents a(n)

   a. individualized teaching method.
   b. within-class ability grouping method.
   c. between-class ability grouping method.
   d. mastery-based learning model.

2. Ms. Fenster divides her math class into three ability groups according to how well they score on an initial exam. The orientation being used is

   a. within-class ability grouping
   b. regrouping.
   c. the Joplin Plan.
   d. between-class ability grouping.

3. Between-class ability grouping appears to be ineffective because

   a. grouping is often done according to general ability rather than specific subject tests.
   b. quality of instruction is often lower in low-track classes than in higher tracks.
   c. there may be a stigmatizing effect on low-track students.
   d. all of the above.

4. Research on within-class ability grouping suggests that it is

   a. not more effective than between-class ability grouping.
   b. detrimental to high-ability students but helpful to low-ability students.
   c. more effective when large rather than small numbers of ability groups are used.
   d. effective for students at all ability levels.

5. In using the Ability-Grouped Active Teaching method, it is recommended that

   a. IQ scores be used for placement.
   b. from three to four teaching groups be established.
   c. once a student is assigned to a particular group, he/she remain in it for at least one semester (half a year).
   d. only about 40% of the students be assigned to the low ability group.

6. Which of the following is true regarding the use of within-class ability grouping in subjects such as social studies and English?

   a. It is generally used as much in those subjects as in math and reading.
   b. An important disadvantage is the creation of unsupervised seatwork time that may not contribute to learning.
   c. Although it is used less than in math and reading, it is actually even more effective.
   d. An important advantage is systematizing the "building block" nature of learning in those subjects.

7. According to Carroll's model, degree of school learning is a function of

   a. ability divided by time allotted.
   b. time spent divided by time needed.
   c. ability divided by time spent.
   d. time needed divided by time spent.

8. Reba has a lot of friends and seeks out social interactions. She hates her class in social studies, however. They are doing map reading and she becomes confused in trying to interrelate the information shown about cities and their geographic locations. One might infer Reba's learning style to be

   a. field independent.
   b. field dependent.
   c. impulsive.
   d. reflective.

9. Enrichment activities are used to

   a. orient students to mastery learning.
   b. help students who have failed to reach criterion on a formative quiz.
   c. help students who have failed to reach criterion on a summative quiz.
   d. keep students who have reached criterion usefully occupied.

10. Under a mastery learning model, grading is based on

a. the time required to read criterion.
b. one's position on the summative test relative to others.
c. one's success or failure at reaching the criterion.
d. the number of points one scores above or below the criterion.

11. Probably the strongest and most adaptive form of individualized instruction is

a. the Keller Plan.
b. mastery learning.
c. computer-assisted instruction.
d. one-to-one tutoring.

12. Which of the following statements about programmed instruction is true?

a. It is no longer used today.
b. It has been found in research studies to be consistently more effective than conventional methods.
c. It is rarely used today as primary instruction, but is often applied as a supplement.
d. It varies the content of lessons but forces students to work at essentially the same pace.

13. In which one of the following are learning groups composed of students having <u>similar</u> abilities?

a. Team Assisted Individualization
b. Joplin Plan
c. Cooperative Integrated Reading and Composition
d. Ability-Grouped Active Teaching

14. Research on Team Assisted Individualization has shown it to be

a. less effective than conventional methods in increasing achievement.
b. no more effective than conventional methods in increasing achievement.
c. more effective than conventional methods in increasing achievement.

15. When peer tutoring is correctly employed, the usual effect is that

a. tutors benefit but tutees do not.
b. tutees benefit but tutors do not.
c. both tutors and tutees benefit.
d. neither tutors nor tutees benefit.

16. PLATO is the name given to a

   a. large-scale CAI system using a central computer.
   b. microcomputer developed by the Minnesota Educational Computing Consortium for school applications.
   c. simulation program that models logical thinking.
   d. computer-management system that does grading and record-keeping.

17. The most widely used type of CAI software is _____ programs.

   a. simulation
   b. tutorial
   c. drill-and-practice
   d. utility

18. The type of program that most closely resembles teacher dialogue with students is

   a. simulation.
   b. tutorial.
   c. drill-and-practice.
   d. utility.

19. Positive effects of CAI appear to be especially strong for

   a. college students.
   b. low achievers.
   c. high school students.
   d. females.

20. The notion that learning programming increases problem solving ability

   a. remains to be verified in research.
   b. is strongly denounced in the writings of Seymour Papert.
   c. has been extensively tested using BASIC and FORTRAN languages.
   d. all of the above.

<u>APPLICATION:</u> Individualized Courses

Shown below are excerpts from a course outline used in a college-level statistics course taught by the author of this study guide. Read the procedure and respond to the following questions:

A. What are your general reactions to this course structure? Would you prefer to take a course this way or through a traditional lecture-type approach?

B. What advantages would the individualized structure provide?

C. What disadvantages?

D. What are your intuitive "projections" for a course of this type relative to a traditional course regarding (1) how much is learned, (2) how quickly the course is completed, (3) what type of student benefits most and what type benefits least, and (4) how students would react?

Course Procedure

For all practical purposes, the first day of class will be the last day of class. In other words, following an initial orientation session, we will not meet again formally as a group. However, students will probably meet with the instructor numerous times during the semester on an individual basis. The exact number of meetings will be left to the discretion of the student as will almost everything else relating to the course. The instructor will serve primarily as a tutor and facilitator with his responsibilities viewed as a) monitoring student progress, b) making advice and remediation available, and c) administering and grading examinations.

As an overview, the course will be organized into 10 units all of which are presented in the textbook. Each unit includes a statement of specific objectives followed by instruction, and "capped off" with a practice posttest. It is recommended that you try to solve all practice problems and then check the accuracy of your answers in the answer section. If you have difficulty understanding any part of the material, you are strongly encouraged to attend one of the "help-sessions" scheduled during the week, or to call and arrange an appointment. At that time, the instructor or an assistant will attempt to provide the needed clarification. Students who do not seek such assistance when problems arise will obviously be cheating themselves and will receive little sympathy (help sessions are an essential component of the present course structure). Once you complete a unit, attend one of the help-sessions for the purpose of taking the corresponding mastery test. If you receive a score of 80 points or above, credit for the unit will be awarded and you will be allowed to proceed to the next unit. If you do not receive a score of at least 80 points, it will be necessary for you to take a retest in order to receive credit. You will be permitted to take as many retests as required and as time permits.

Grades will be determined according to the number of units you complete. Scores on individual tests will not be added together or averaged. All that matters is that on each test you reach the criterion of 80 points.

Units Completed (by final exam day)	Grade
I - X	A
I - VII	B
I - VI	C
I - III	D

APPLICATION: Comparing Instructional Methods

Choosing between instructional methods always involves a trade-off between positive and negative features of the different options. Identify a subject area (mathematics, English, etc.) and suppose that you had the option of teaching it (say, for a one-week period) using conventional instruction (CI), mastery learning (ML), or computer-assisted instruction (CAI). Assume that suitable instructional materials are available for the latter two methods. Use the chart below to evaluate and compare attributes of these methods. Then identify and briefly defend the method you prefer.

Subject Area:______________________________________

	METHOD		
Attribute	CI	ML	CAI
Pacing			
Adaptiveness to Learning Needs			
Motivational Effects			
Suitability for Knowledge (memorization) Outcomes			
Suitability for Higher-Order Outcomes (Comprehension, Application, etc.)			
Adaptiveness to Emotional Needs			
Induces Active Learning			
Provides Response Feedback			
Provides Reinforcement			
Amount of Work for Teacher			

APPLICATION: Field Experience

Visit a class in which grouping is used for reading, mathematics, or some other subject. Observe and informally evaluate how the grouping procedure is managed with regard to: (a) number of groups, (b) size of groups, (c) seating arrangements, (d) seatwork, (e) teaching (whole class, group only, individual), (f) distribution of instructional resources, and (g) discipline.

APPLICATION: Mastery Learning

Mr. Herman, a middle-school math teacher, reads an article describing the Mastery Learning approach. He finds the approach quite appealing, but in fancying himself an individualist, feels that he could definitely make some changes that would make the method even stronger. Unfortunately, Mr. Herman sometimes becomes more involved with generating ideas than with thoughtfully considering how they are likely to work. He decides to leave that task to you. Presented below is the list. React to each suggestion indicating whether you feel it would strengthen or weaken the effectiveness of mastery learning.

Mr. Herman's list:

A. Eliminate formative quizzes and use only summative tests.

B. Give students a set amount of time to complete a unit, after which their grade is lowered, and they can move on to the next.

C. Set the mastery criterion at 50 percent.

D. Keep the formative quizzes but make them count toward the student's final grade.

E. Eliminate enrichment activities; have successful students proceed to the next unit.

F. Have students take the summative tests in pairs.

G. Raise the mastery criterion on all quizzes to 100 percent.

APPLICATION: Computers in Education

Most schools and colleges of education today have software libraries. Examine the listings and descriptions (if available) of CAI software available at your institution.

A. Which type of CAI (drill-and-practice, tutorials, simulations, games) appears to be most frequently represented?

B. Select an example from each software category and briefly review it. What appears to be its strong and weak features relative to print (textbook or workbook) lessons?

C. Examine the programs on the EDUCATIONAL PSYCHOLOGY COMPUTER DISK for your text (if available) and classify them into the different CAI categories. Evaluate their strengths and weaknesses in extending or altering what can be achieved from print materials.

ESSAY/DISCUSSION

1. Differentiate between within- and between-class ability grouping. Which orientation do you personally favor and for what reasons?

2. Define what is meant by "learning style" and give examples of at least two different types discussed in your text.

3. List and discuss the major elements of the Ability-Grouped Active Teaching orientation.

4. Discuss how the use of grouping techniques might differ in the case of teaching reading relative to teaching mathematics.

5. The main premise of mastery learning is that given additional instructional time, students who might not otherwise achieve mastery should be able to reach achievement levels typically attained by only the most able students. Discuss your views on the practicality of this idea. Specifically, can it be applied in typical classrooms? What procedural adjustments need to be made to use mastery learning within a fixed time period, such as a semester or a school year?

6. Suppose that you are hired to teach a familiar subject to adults. Since the students' work schedules make it difficult for them all to attend class at one specified time, it is recommended that you individualize the course. Discuss how such an individualized orientation might be developed and used with regard to: (a) instructional material, (b) testing, (c) student advancement through lessons, (d) student-instructor interactions, and (e) grading.

7. Describe and differentiate between each of the following types of CAI programs: (a) tutorial, (b) drill-and-practice, (c) simulation, and (d) games.

ANSWERS

Matching Warm-ups

Quiz 1

a. 2 (275)
b. 4 (275)
c. 1 (275)
d. 3 (275)

Quiz 2

a. 4 (282)
b. 1 (288)
c. 8 (278)
d. 2 (288)
e. 3 (295)
f. 7 (300)
g. 5 (297)

Quiz 3

a. 3 (301)
b. 1 (282)
c. 5 (275)
d. 2 (288)
e. 7 (306)
f. 6 (290)
g. 4 (288)
h. 1 (296)

Key Terms

1. B (275)
2. Z (302)
3. G (278)
4. O (292)
5. X (300)
6. E (275)
7. Y (302)
8. S (295)
9. Q (293)
10. T (295)
11. C;D (275)
12. U (296)
13. P (292)
14. I (279)
15. W (300)
16. J (282)
17. CC (303)
18. H (278)
19. N (292)
20. M (288)
21. V (297)
22. L (286)
23. EE (305)
24. AA (303)
25. BB (303)
26. DD (304)
27. R (293)
28. A (274)
29. F (276)
30. K (288)

Completion Questions

1. reflective (275)
2. field-dependent (275)
3. within-class ability grouping (279)
4. between-class ability grouping (276)
5. mixed-ability (278)
6. reading; math (281)
7. two (279; 281)
8. the Missouri Mathematics Program (282)
9. seatwork (283-285)
10. Cooperative Integrated Reading and Composition (288)
11. time needed (288)
12. time (288-289)
13. Keller Plan (290)
14. summative (292)
15. formative (292)
16. corrective instruction (293)
17. enrichment activities (293)
18. programmed instruction (295)
19. Team Assisted Individualization (296)
20. cross-age (297)
21. PLATO (302)
22. tutorial (303)
23. branching; linear (303)
24. simulation (304)
25. utility (305)
26. Logo (306)

Multiple-Choice

1. c (274)
2. a (279)
3. d (277)
4. d (279)
5. d (282)
6. b (281)
7. b (288)
8. b (275)
9. d (293)
10. c (289-290)
11. d (295)
12. c (296)
13. d (275)
14. c (297)
15. c (299)
16. a (302)
17. c (302)
18. b (303)
19. b (305)
20. a (306)

10 Motivation

CHAPTER OUTLINE

I. Meaning and Importance of Motivation

II. Theories of Motivation
- A. Motivation and reinforcers
  1. Behavioral interpretations
  2. Motivation as an explanation of behavior
- B. Rewards and reinforcers
  1. Social definitions
  2. Individual differences in motivation histories
  3. Behavior as a product of competing motivations
- C. Motivation and needs
  1. Self-actualization
  2. Implications of Maslow's hierarchy of needs for education
- D. Teachers on teaching: Increasing student motivation
- E. Cognitive dissonance
  1. Festinger's cognitive dissonance theory
  2. Experimental findings on cognitive dissonance effects
  3. Importance of cognitive dissonance for education
- F. Attribution theory
  1. Comparison to dissonance theory
  2. Locus of control
  3. Ability, effort, task difficulty, and luck as explanations of achievement
  4. Importance of attributions for education
- G. Motivation and personality
  1. The stability of motivational drives

2. Situational motivation-related personality characteristics
3. Patterns of motivation

H. Achievement motivation
1. Relationship to success in school
2. Seeking success as opposed to avoiding failure
3. Learning versus performance goals

I. Learned helplessness

J. Achievement motivation and attribution training
1. Programs that promote change
2. Origins and pawns
3. Training students to be origins

K. Expectancy theories of motivation
1. "Expectancy-valence" model
2. A formulation to predict motivation for exerting maximum effort
3. Importance of expectancy theory for education

L. Teacher and student expectations
1. Rosenthal and Jacobson's findings
2. Additional research findings
3. Five-step process
4. Communicating positive expectations

M. Teachers on teaching: Effects of achievement and expectations

III. Incentives for Learning

A. Intrinsic and extrinsic motivation
1. Intrinsic incentives
2. Extrinsic incentives
3. Do extrinsic rewards destroy intrinsic motivation?

B. Enhancing intrinsic motivation
1. Whetting students' appetites for knowledge
2. Maintaining curiosity
3. Interesting and varied presentation modes
4. Games and simulations

C. Incentives for learning: Basic principles
1. Clear expectations
2. Clarity and immediacy of feedback
3. Frequency of assessment, feedback, and reward
4. Value of rewards
5. Availability of rewards

D. Teachers on teaching: Incentives for learning

E. Classroom rewards
1. Traditional classroom rewards
2. Long-term vs. short-term rewards

F. Praise
1. Making rewards contingent, specific, and credible
2. Characteristics of effective and ineffective praise

G. Feedback
1. Feedback as information
2. Feedback as incentives

H. Grades as incentives
   1. Evaluations, feedback, and incentives
   2. Parental valuing of grades
I. Goal setting
   1. Individualized Guided Motivation (IGM)
   2. Research on IGM

IV. Rewarding Effort and Improvement
   A. Theory into practice: Individual Learning Expectations (ILE)
      1. Instruction
      2. Quizzes
      3. Initial base scores
      4. Improvement points
      5. Feedback to students
      6. Certificates
      7. Recomputing base scores
      8. Improvement points and grades
   B. Behavior modification and home-based reinforcement strategies
   C. Cooperation and competition
      1. Goal structures of classrooms
      2. Cooperative and competitive goal structures
   D. Cooperative learning methods
      1. Cooperative learning groups in classes
      2. Research applications and results
   E. Theory into practice: Student Teams-Achievement Divisions (STAD)
      1. Assigning students to teams
      2. Preparing materials
      3. Schedule of activities
      4. Teach
      5. Team study
      6. Test
      7. Figuring individual and team scores
      8. Recognizing team accomplishments
      9. Changing teams

Summary/Study Questions/Suggested Readings

CHAPTER OBJECTIVES

1. Give examples of basic needs--those that people are motivated to meet for survival--and of growth needs.
2. Describe the implications for a person of attributing success or failure to internal or external factors.
3. Define achievement motivation and describe its implications for education.

4. Give examples of how the expectations that teachers have for students can affect student motivation.
5. Present lessons that students will be motivated to learn.

MATCHING WARM-UPS

Match the numbers of the descriptions on the right to the corresponding items on the left. A given item from the right column may be used more than once or not at all.

Quiz 1: Attribution Theory

_____	a. Luck	1. internal-stable
_____	b. Effort	2. external-unstable
_____	c. Ability	3. external-stable
_____	d. Task Difficulty	4. internal-unstable

Quiz 2: Notable Names

_____	a. Attribution theory	1. Festinger
_____	b. Achievement motivation	2. Bandura
_____	c. Hierarchy of needs	3. Rotter
_____	d. Cognitive dissonance	4. Weiner
_____	e. Epistemic curiosity	5. Slavin
_____	f. Performance vs. learning goals	6. Berlyne
_____	g. Expectancy-valence model	7. DeCharms
_____	h. Student Teams-Achievement Divisions	8. Maslow
_____	i. Locus of control	9. Atkinson and McClelland
_____	j. "Origins" and "pawns"	10. Dweck
		11. Edwards

KEY TERMS

Fill in the blanks below with the letter identifying the following concepts. Each concept is used one time only.

A. Motivation	J. Learning goals
B. Deficiency needs	K. Performance goals
C. Growth needs	L. Learned helplessness
D. Self-actualization	M. Expectancy-valance theory
E. Cognitive dissonance theory	N. Intrinsic incentive
F. Attribution theory	O. Extrinsic incentive
G. Locus of control	P. Individual Learning Expectations
H. Achievement motivation	Q. Goal structure
I. Thematic Apperception Test	R. Cooperative learning

1. Students who are motivated to increase their skillls, regardless of the grades they receive, are said to have _____.

2. Each classroom has a different _____ by placing certain degrees of emphasis on competitive vs. cooperative relationships.

3. A system in which students are rewarded on the basis of improvement is _____.

4. Needs that can never be satisfied completely, such as the need to know and understand things, to appreciate beauty, or to appreciate others, are referred to as _____ needs.

5. Factors that intensify and direct behavior toward a specific goal make up a person's _____.

6. A person with high _____ tends to strive for success on goal-oriented tasks based on skill.

7. The type of need defined by Maslow as "the desire to become everything that one is capable of becoming" is _____.

8. The success of the group determines the reward received by each member under a(n) _____ structure.

9. A personality trait that concerns whether success or failure is attributed to internal or external factors is _____.

10. An individual's deeply held beliefs are challenged in a speech that he hears from a respected authority. The resultant tension or discomfort the listener experiences is explained by _____.

11. A(n) _____ is present when tasks are inherently interesting to individuals; for uninteresting tasks, however, a(n) _____ may need to be provided through reinforcers such as recognition or prizes.

12. The perception that failure is inevitable no matter what actions are taken is called _____.

13. Understanding how individuals explain personal successes and failures is the subject of _____.

14. The _____ is based on the idea that an individual's descriptions of ambiguous pictures tend to convey personality characteristics such as achievement motivation or affiliation motivation.

15. A mathematical model that relates individuals' motivation levels to their perceptions of their chances of success is the _____.

16. Needs that are critical to physical and psychological well-being, such as food, shelter, and safety, are _____.

17. Students motivated to earn recognition regardless of how much they learn are said to have _____.

COMPLETION QUESTIONS

1. Needs that are critical to survival or physical well-being are called _____ needs; those involving knowing or understanding are called _____ needs.

2. Two ways that motivations vary are _____ and _____.

3. A student who is hungry will probably not learn very effectively. The type of need, from Maslow, represented by the hunger is _____.

4. A student who is caught stealing money from another student attempts to rationalize his behavior by saying "Joey needed to be taught to hide his money." This excuse suggests the presence of a type of intellectual discomfort called _____.

5. Mike attributes his failing grade to "bad luck" in answering, thus reflecting a(n) _____ locus of control in this situation.

6. Bob attributes his failing grade to his lack of effort in studying, thus reflecting a(n) _____ locus of control.

7. Teachers who want to convey that all students can succeed should emphasize that high achievement is mostly dependent on _____, an internal but alterable attribution.

8. "Luck" is a(n) _____ -_____ type of attribution.

9. Based on Atkinson's and McClelland's work, achievement motivation takes two forms: seeking success and _____.

10. Tim receives a grade of A on the algebra test. Tim is pleased because now he will move ahead of Jason to the number 2 position in class. Tim could be described as being motivated by _____ goals.

11. Brenda also receives an A on the algebra test. Her reaction is "Wow, I've really become good at this stuff!" She could be described as being motivated by _____ goals.

12. DeCharms calls people who take control over their own fate _____, and those who do not _____.

13. A mathematical formula for predicting motivation based on individuals' estimations of their chances of success is called an _____ model.

14. In the mathematical predictive model (Item #13), the two major types of expectations which influence motivation are _____ and _____.

15. As perceived probability of success under maximum effort increases, overall motivation would tend to _____. When perceived probability of success under minimum effort increases, overall motivation would tend to _____.

16. Teacher _____ communicate to the student what behaviors are anticipated, and thus serve to promote those very behaviors.

17. Tasks that are naturally interesting to a student provide _____ incentive.

18. Praise is considered effective to the extent that it is _____, contingent, and _____.

19. Three functions of grades and grading systems are (1) evaluations, (2) _____, and (3) _____.

20. The Individual Learning Expectations System rewards students for _____ rather than for surpassing others.

21. A group structure in which students help one another to maximize group performance is called _____ learning.

22. In the _____ model, team scores are based on individual scores and provide the basis for recognition of success.

MULTIPLE-CHOICE

Select the best answer for each of the following items.

1. Bill excitedly raises his hand in class, trying to answer as many questions as possible. One can confidently infer that Bill is motivated to

    a. increase his learning of the subject.
    b. demonstrate his knowledge to classmates.
    c. obtain recognition from the teacher.
    d. none of these can be confidently assumed.

2. Based on Maslow's hierarchy, which of the following needs, if presently unsatisfied, would an individual attempt to fulfill first?

    a. Esteem needs
    b. Physiological needs
    c. Belongingness and love needs
    d. Safety needs

3. Which of the following descriptions regarding "growth needs" is <u>correct?</u>

   a. The more one attends to them, the greater the motivation to meet or satisfy them may become.
   b. They are mainly concentrated at the bottom (lower part) of Maslow's hierarchy.
   c. Once they are completely satisfied, the tendency is to concentrate on deficiency needs.
   d. Esteem needs are an example.

4. Self-actualization can be described as

   a. a deficiency need.
   b. the need most critical to good adjustment in school situations.
   c. the motivation to avoid failure in relationships with others.
   d. a need requiring adequate satisfaction of all other needs.

5. Which of the following is a correct implication of Maslow's hierarchy for education?

   a. A student with low self-esteem will probably have little motivation to belong to and be liked by a group.
   b. A student who is feeling ill or unsafe may show little interest in academic performances.
   c. Failure to satisfy aesthetic needs will prevent a student from having high self-esteem.
   d. A student who is frustrated in her search for knowledge may show little interest in her physiological well-being.

6. One group of students (Group A) is told that if they read a certain book at home, they will receive extra credit and be excused from three subsequent reading assignments. Group B is simply encouraged to read the same book, without any special incentives. Based on cognitive dissonance theory, one might predict that

   a. Group B members would describe the book as more interesting than would Group A members.
   b. Group B members would be less likely than Group A members to read on their own in the future.
   c. Group B and Group A members would report about the same amount of interest in the book.
   d. Group A members would describe the book as more interesting than would Group B members.

7. Which of the following terms describes a very common outcome when individuals experience cognitive dissonance?

   a. Epistemic curiosity
   b. Affiliation need
   c. Learned helplessness
   d. Rationalization

8. A person with a high internal locus of control

   a. tends to attribute success to chance, luck, or fate.
   b. is likely to perform better in school than those having a low internal locus of control.
   c. is likely to deny the importance of success or failure in school.
   d. needs to see a doctor immediately.

9. Which of the following pairs represent attributions that are external to the individual?

   a. Task difficulty and effort
   b. Effort and ability
   c. Ability and luck
   d. Luck and task difficulty

10. Which of the following statements by students represents an internal but alterable type of attribution?

   a. "I blew the test because I didn't study at all."
   b. "I aced that test since I'm naturally brilliant."
   c. "Got lucky I guess on that one. Never expected a B+."
   d. "How can I expect to pass? His exams are ridiculously hard."

11. The computer programming quizzes are returned, and the grades are low for just about everyone, even though much progress has been made. Which type of student would be most debilitated by his/her low grade?

   a. A success-seeker
   b. One having an external locus of control
   c. One having performance goals
   d. One having learning goals

12. In reviewing possible topics for science fair projects, the teacher classifies different groups as "fairly easy," "moderate in difficulty," and "very difficult." A student who is high in failure avoidance motivation might be expected to select

   a. a fairly easy topic.
   b. a very difficult topic.
   c. a moderately difficult topic.
   d. either a. or b.

13. In the same situation described in Item 12, a student who is high in success-seeking motivation might be expected to select

    a. a fairly easy topic.
    b. a very difficult topic.
    c. a moderately difficult topic.
    d. either a. or b.

14. The main implication of research on achievement motivation training is that such programs

    a. can be effective on both a short-term and long-term basis.
    b. cannot change long-standing patterns of low achievement motivation in the typical student.
    c. work well with upper- and middle-class students, but poorly with lower-class students.
    d. are helpful only while the program is operating.

15. According to expectancy-valance models of motivation, motivation is likely to increase as

    a. perceived probability of success under minimum effort increases.
    b. incentive value of success decreases.
    c. perceived probability of success under maximum effort decreases.
    d. perceived probability of success under maximum effort increases.

16. Relative to the findings from early, highly controlled studies, recent findings concerning the effects of rewards on school-like tasks suggest that

    a. extrinsic rewards consistently lower intrinsic motivation.
    b. extrinsic rewards may raise intrinsic motivation when contingent upon the quality of performance.
    c. intrinsic motivation is likely to increase the incentive value of extrinsic rewards when tasks are relatively easy.
    d. extrinsic rewards consistently raise intrinsic motivation, regardless of task difficulty.

17. Ms. Saunders glances at Marta and remembers how well Marta has been doing her homework assignments. She ways, "Marta, I'm pleased with you this year." Although Marta is happy about the comment, Ms. Saunders nevertheless failed to make her praise

    a. contingent.
    b. specific.
    c. available.
    d. credible.

18. Experiments comparing graded and ungraded classes mostly show

a. no differences between these orientations.
b. higher performance in the graded classes.
c. higher performance in the ungraded classes.
d. that low-achievers benefit more from graded classes and high-achievers from ungraded classes.

19. The main emphasis of the Individual Learning Expectations (ILE) system is

a. administering concrete rewards ("tokens") for good performance.
b. grading on the basis of grade level or age-group norms.
c. grading on the basis of individual improvement.
d. team teaching, open classrooms, and no formal assignment of grades.

20. Which of the following shows a correct pairing between goal structure and grading philosophy?

a. Individualized: "If some succeed, others must fail."
b. Cooperation: "One student's success has no bearing on another's fate."
c. Competition: "All succeed or all fail."
d. None is correct.

APPLICATION: Dealing With Cognitive Dissonance

Answer the following questions for each of the episodes below:

1. Where is cognitive dissonance likely to occur?
2. What might be some negative effects on future behaviors?
3. How might the authority figure (parent or teacher) intervene to prevent (or help reverse) those undesirable changes?

A. Bobby Sloan, who is 13 years old, loves being outdoors even when work is involved. One of his favorite work activities, which he performs diligently every week, is to mow and manicure the lawn in front of his house. His parents (naturally) are quite pleased by this activity and always make an effort to be very complementary about the finished product. One day, his father is so pleased that he gives Bobby ten dollars "just for being such an enthusiastic worker." Bobby, though surprised, is glad to accept since he very much wants to buy a record album.

The next week Bobby's father is just as pleased. Digging into his pocket he finds five dollars and gives it to Bobby. Bobby initially thinks it is a ten-dollar bill, but seeing that it is a five-dollar bill isn't really disappointing. That money and the change from last week will purchase another album. The next week Bobby's father again notices the fine job on the lawn, but having no money with him, makes a point of shaking Bobby's hand and profusely congratulating him. But, despite the compliments, Bobby's face falls. He looks at his dad and asks, "Aren't I going to get paid this week?" His father sternly replies, "We don't pay you for doing the lawn. The last few weeks were just one-time bonuses." Bobby hunches his shoulders and goes back to his work. A few weeks later one of the neighbors notices that the Sloan's lawn isn't looking so spectacular any more. He wonders whether it is the very dry weather they are having this year.

B. Tina Morris was proud of her accomplishments on the junior-high gymnastics team. Although last year she barely made the team and rarely got to compete in school meets, this year she had moved up to become (what she thought) one of the team's top four or five performers. She became obsessed with gymnastics and spent much of her day thinking about her events, accomplishments, and friends on the team. One day Mrs. Lewis, the gymnastics coach, told the team that she would select five members to compete in a special meet upstate. Tina's heart began to pound with excitement. She knew that this year she would be one of the five. She excitedly made her way to the bulletin board to examine the names. As she glanced through the list, a sinking feeling rapidly set in. Tears streamed down her cheeks as she ran from the room. The next day Tina was not at practice. Someone said she seemed to have a cold or an allergy that day. No one, not even Mrs. Lewis, knew that at that moment, Tina's locker was empty.

<u>APPLICATION:</u> Motivation and Personality

Read each of the behavioral descriptions presented below. Then analyze each using whatever characterization seems relevant from <u>locus of control</u> theory (internal vs. external), <u>attribution</u> theory (effort, ability, task difficulty, luck), and achievement theory (success seeking vs. failure avoidance). Does the cognitive behavior in each instance seem productive of future high performances on similar tasks?

A. Jill is a straight-A student in English. On her last English theme she received a grade of A+ with the comment from the teacher, "The best in class." Jill describes that success by saying, "I've always been good in English--guess it just comes naturally."

B. Frank falls off the parallel bars in physical education class for the second time in a row. He comments, "I don't understand why they make these bars so slippery. At the Rec Center, the equipment is so much better than here."

C. Jamie completes her computer program and receives many compliments about its appearance and quality from her classmates. She replies, "Thanks but any of you could do the same if you put in the work. Programming involves applying yourself--it's 90% that."

D. During recess, some of the children are shooting baskets in the school yard. Jonathan frequently takes his shots standing either far beyond the free throw line or very close to the basket. In nearly all instances, he misses the far shots and makes the near ones.

E. For the first time ever, Barry is the winner of the spelling bee. He thinks, "Boy, was I lucky. I had no idea what I was doing...guess the correct answers somehow floated into my brain."

F. Andrew presents his "A" test paper to his father to sign. His father is impressed by the good grade since Andrew had previously earned mostly B's. Andrew, however, is thinking "I'm really a 'B' student so this must have been an easy test."

G. Emily receives a "D" in history. She reacts by thinking to herself, "I've always been dumb in history."

H. Sara always gives careful thought in selecting projects to perform for science class. She wants a project that is suitably challenging, but not something that is too difficult to complete successfully. She decides that for this week, a project on sea birds' nests will meet this criterion.

I. Following a loss in a basketball game, the team center is asked his impression. He says, "We lost because we practiced poorly and played poorly. There's no other excuse!"

APPLICATION: Student Teams-Achievement Divisions

Remember Mr. Herman from the last chapter's Applications? He's the middle-school math teacher who likes to read about innovative systems and then think of creative (but not always so thoughtful) ways of changing them. This time his target is STAD. React to each of the following suggestions by Mr. Herman indicating whether you feel it would strengthen or weaken the effectiveness of STAD.

1. Compose the teams of uniform-ability rather than mixed-ability members.

2. Establish half the number of teams by making them consist of 8 rather than 4 members each.

3. Distribute copies of the worksheets to all rather than only some members.

4. Collect the worksheets from students and grade them.

5. Allow students to take the final quiz in pairs.

6. Replace the ILE scoring system with one based on actual scores (not improvement points).

ESSAY/DISCUSSION

1. In earlier chapters you learned about behavioral and cognitive theories of learning. How would motivation be defined by each type of theory? What suggestions might each theory offer regarding possible ways of increasing students' motivation for learning.

2. What is meant by reinforcer? Describe situations in which each of the following stimuli might serve as a reinforcer for one student but not for another.

    a. A test score of 90/100
    b. Ice cream
    c. A field trip to the zoo

3. In recent years there has been considerable controversy regarding the appropriateness of using tax money to subsidize school lunch programs. (One administration exacerbated the conflict immensely by trying to classify ketchup as a vegetable.) Regardless of the financial considerations, evaluate the possible benefits of such programs from the perspective of Maslow's hierarchy. What desirable outcomes might be fostered that would not otherwise occur? (Bonus: should ketchup be considered a vegetable?)

4. The classic Festinger (1957) experiment produced quite interesting results. What is the meaning of those results for classroom learning? Construct or identify an applied example in which students are treated by a teacher much like the "$20" group was in the experiment.

5. What are possible disadvantages of internal-stable attributions such as "I succeeded because I am smart,"" or "I failed because I am dumb." What can a teacher do to foster more productive sets of beliefs (particularly in the latter case) when he/she views such self-perceptions as justified.

6. Explain, using examples, how teacher expectations can become self-fulfilling prophesies. Do you feel it is possible for group achievement to be drastically increased or decreased through communication of such expectancies?

7. Discuss your reactions to the Individual Learning Expectations (ILE) system. What do you see as its possible advantages and disadvantages? Do you feel it would be more or less helpful to particular types of students? Explain.

ANSWERS

Matching Warm-Ups

Quiz 1

a. 2 (319-320)
b. 4 (319-320)
c. 1 (319-320)
d. 3 (319-320)

Quiz 2

a. 4 (319)
b. 9 (323)
c. 8 (314)
d. 1 (317)
e. 6 (333)
f. 10 (324)
g. 11 (326)
h. 5 (346)
i. 3 (320)
j. 7 (325)

Key Terms

1. J (324)
2. Q (345)
3. P (342)
4. C (314)
5. A (311)
6. H (323)
7. D (314)
8. R (345)
9. G (320)
10. E (317)
11. N,O (331)
12. L (325)
13. F (319)
14. I (322)
15. M (326)
16. B (314)
17. K (324)

Completion Questions

1. deficiency; growth (314)
2. intensity; direction (311)
3. physiological (314-315)
4. cognitive dissonance (317)
5. external (320)
6. internal (320)
7. effort (321)
8. external-unstable (321)
9. avoiding failure (323)
10. performance (324)
11. learning (324)
12. origins, pawns (325)
13. expectancy-valance (326)
14. perceived probability of success, incentive value (326)
15. increase; decrease (326-327)
16. expectations (328)
17. intrinsic (331)
18. specific; credible (340)
19. feedback; incentives (341)
20. improvement (342)
21. cooperative (345)
22. Student Teams-Achievement Divisions (346)

Multiple-Choice

1.	d (311)	11.	c (324)
2.	b (314-315)	12.	d (323)
3.	a (314)	13.	c (323)
4.	d (314)	14.	a (325)
5.	b (315)	15.	d (326)
6.	a (318)	16.	b (332)
7.	d (318)	17.	b (339)
8.	b (320)	18.	b (341)
9.	d (319)	19.	c (342-343)
10.	a (319-321)	20.	d (345)

Application: Motivation and Personality

A. ability attribution; internal locus of control
B. task difficulty attribution; external locus of control
C. effort attribution; internal locus of control
D. failure avoidance
E. luck attribution; external locus of control
F. task difficulty attribution; external locus of control
G. ability attribution; internal locus of control
H. success seeking
I. effort attribution; internal locus of control

11 Classroom Management and Discipline

CHAPTER OUTLINE

I Time and Learning
- A. Where does time go?
  1. Treating time as a limited resource
  2. Maximizing periods of instruction
- B. Allocated time for instruction
  1. Avoiding late starts, early finishes
  2. Avoiding interruptions
  3. Handling routine procedures smoothly and quickly
  4. Minimizing time spent on discipline
- C. Engaged time
  1. Maintaining momentum and smoothness of instruction
  2. Managing transitions
  3. Maintaining group focus during lessons
  4. Maintaining group focus during seatwork
  5. Withitness
  6. Overlapping
- D. Engaged time vs. engaging instruction: A caution
- E. Classroom rules and behavior
  1. Starting the year properly
  2. Setting class rules
- F. Teachers on teaching: Classroom management
- G. Theory into practice: Management concerns over the school years
  1. Elementary school (K-5)
  2. Middle/junior high school grades (5-9)
  3. High school grades (9-12)
- H. Teachers on teaching: Management at different grade levels

II. Discipline
- A. Structure and freedom
- B. Managing routine behavior
  - 1. Minor disruptions need to be minimized
  - 2. The principle of least intervention
    - a. Prevention
    - b. Nonverbal cues
    - c. Praise incompatible behavior
    - d. Praise other students
    - f. Repeated reminders
    - g. Applying consequences
- C. Teachers on teaching: Misconduct and discipline
- D. Managing more serious behavior problems

III. Behavior Modification
- A. What maintains student misbehavior?
  - 1. Teacher's attention
  - 2. Peers' attention
  - 3. Release from boredom, frustration, or fatigue

IV. Behavior Modification and Classroom Management
- A. Individual behavior modification strategies
  - 1. Identify target behavior(s) and reinforcer(s)
  - 2. Establish a baseline for the target behavior
  - 3. Decide on a reinforcer and a criterion for reinforcement
  - 4. If necessary, decide on punishers and criteria for punishment
  - 5. Observe behavior and compare to baseline
  - 6. When the behavior management program is working, reduce the frequency of reinforcement
- B. Home-based reinforcement
  - 1. Advantages over other behavior management strategies
  - 2. Example of daily report card program
- C. Theory into practice: Daily report cards
  - 1. Decide on behaviors to include in the daily report card
  - 2. Explain the program to parents
  - 3. When behavior improves, reduce the frequency of the report
- D. Group contingencies
  - 1. Based on behavior of entire group
  - 2. Examples of group contingency programs
- E. Teachers on teaching: Solving discipline problems
- F. Theory into practice: Group contingency programs
  - 1. Decide which behaviors will be reinforced
  - 2. Set up a point system
  - 3. Consider deducting points for serious behavior
  - 4. When behavior improves, reduce the frequency of the points and reinforcers
  - 5. Combine group and individual contingencies if necessary
- G. Ethics of behavior modification

V. Delinquency

A. Preventing delinquency

1. Rules must be clearly expressed and consistently enforced
2. Truancy must be reduced by any means possible
3. Tracking should be avoided if possible
4. The curriculum should be differentiated
5. Behavior modification-based classroom management strategies should be used
6. Involve the student's home in response to serious behavior
7. Avoid the use of suspension and expulsion as punishment
8. When punishment is applied, it should be brief
9. After punishment, reintegrate the student

VI. Delinquency

A. Preventing delinquency

1. Rules must be clearly expressed and consistently enforced
2. Truancy must be reduced by any means possible
3. Tracking should be avoided if possible
4. The curriculum should be differentiated
5. Behavior modification-based classroom management strategies should be used
6. Involve the student's home in response to serious misbehavior
7. Avoid the use of suspension and expulsion as punishment
8. When punishment is applied, it should be brief
9. After punishment, reintegrate the student

Summary/Study Questions/Suggested Readings

CHAPTER OBJECTIVES

1. Plan lessons that make the best use of classroom time.
2. Help students focus on lesson presentations and seatwork.
3. List three reinforcers of student misbehavior.
4. Prevent most minor incidents of misconduct from disrupting lesson presentations.
5. Use strategies of behavior modification to improve student behavior

MATCHING WARM-UPS

Match the numbers of the descriptions on the right to the corresponding items on the left. A given item from the right column may be used more than once or not at all.

Quiz 1: Effective Management Practices

_____ a.	Momentum	1.	Choral responses
_____ b.	Smoothness	2.	Attending to several activities at once
_____ c.	Accountability	3.	Questioning strategies
_____ d.	Group alerting	4.	Few slowdowns
_____ e.	Withitness	5.	"Eyes in the back of one's head"
_____ f.	Overlapping	6.	No "jumps," "jarring breaks"

Quiz 2: The Principle of Least Intervention

_____ a.	Prevention	1.	Moving close to a student
_____ b.	Nonverbal cues	2.	"Molly, I like it when you're so polite"
_____ c.	Praise incompatible behavior	3.	The broken record approach
_____ d.	Praise others	4.	"It's pleasing to see Tom and Brenda working so well"
_____ e.	Simple verbal reminder	5.	"Duane, you'll have to lose 10 min. of study hall for talking"
_____ f.	Repeated reminders	6.	A lively lesson
_____ g.	Applying consequences	7.	"Alicia, do your work quietly"

KEY TERMS

Fill in the blanks below with the letters identifying the following concepts. Each concept is used one time only.

A. Engaged time
B. Allocated time
C. Group alerting
D. Withitness
E. Overlapping
F. Group contingencies
G. Time-out
H. Home-based reinforcement

1. The administration of rewards by parents to modify children's behavior is a major part of _____ programs.

2. The degree to which teachers maintain awareness of students' behavior at all times is called _____.

3. Strategies that reward an entire class for following rules involve the use of _____.

4. Questioning strategies that maintain students' attention serve the function of _____.

5. Teachers give _____ to misbehaving students to remove them from the view of their classmates.

6. The number of minutes actually spent learning comprises _____.

7. The number of minutes during which students have an opportunity to learn comprises _____.

8. A teacher who is able to monitor several different students' behaviors at one time is demonstrating _____.

COMPLETION QUESTIONS

1. The time that a teacher makes available for learning is called _____ time.

2. Time on task or _____ time refers to the number of minutes actually spent learning.

3. Good teachers attempt to maintain _____ by avoiding interruptions or slowdowns.

4. During recitation sessions, good teachers hold their classes _____ by requesting choral responding and monitoring individual performances.

5. Group _____ is used to keep students "on their toes" by calling on them to respond, creating suspense, and so on.

6. Teachers possessing _____ maintain and indicate constant awareness of students' behavior.

7. Teachers do a good job of _____ when they can attend to behavior problems while continuing with a lesson.

8. The principle of _____ emphasizes the correction of misbehavior using the simplest most unobtrusive method that can work.

9. While Johnny pulls Arthur's suspenders, Ms. Ortez raises her eyebrows disapprovingly. She has used a _____ cue to let Johnny, but few others, know that she is aware of the misbehavior.

10. An effective strategy for discipline is to praise behaviors that are _____ with the misbehavior.

11. The specific strategy in which teachers continually repeat a request until the student complies is called the _____.

12. When students appear to misbehave to gain the teacher's attention, a usually effective strategy is to _____ the misbehavior.

13. All students benefit from their classmates' good behavior and forfeit rewards from classmates' misbehavior under a _____ plan.

14. The first step in a systematic behavior modification program is to identify the _____ and reinforcers.

15. A form of punishment which is sometimes illegal and rarely justified is _____ punishment.

16. A form of punishment in which the misbehaving student is removed from the view of other students is called _____.

17. In _____ reinforcement strategies, parents receive daily or weekly "report cards," and are awarded privileges on the basis of the reports.

18. In dealing with delinquent students, _____ should be avoided because it often increases truancy problems by making students fall further behind in their work.

19. A teacher who awards free time to any student who turns in correct homework is using _____.

MULTIPLE-CHOICE

1. Which of the following is a likely outcome of frequently disciplining students during lessons?

   a. Reduction of allocated time; no effect on engaged time
   b. Reduction of engaged time; no effect on allocated time
   c. Reduction of both allocated and engaged time
   d. No effect on either allocated or engaged time

2. The time measure assumed to have the greatest impact on learning is _____ time.

   a. allocated
   b. instructional
   c. clock
   d. engaged

3. Ms. Winston says to the class, "Now I will add sodium to the solution. What do you think we'll see?" According to Kounin, this is an example of

   a. group alerting.
   b. managing transitions.
   c. maintaining momentum.
   d. demonstrating withitness.

4. Teachers who appear to "have eyes in back of their heads" would be described by Kounin as

   a. maintaining group focus.
   b. holding students accountable.
   c. maintaining momentum.
   d. demonstrating withitness.

5. In beginning the year, teachers are advised to do all of the following EXCEPT

   a. break students into ability groups and discuss rules separately with each group.
   b. teach students specific procedures, such as how to line up, respond to a bell, etc.
   c. use simple enjoyable tasks for the first lessons.
   d. devise a clear, specific plan for introducing class rules.

6. Which of the following statements regarding the establishment of class rules is false?

   a. Rules should be seen as fair by students.
   b. Rules should be deliberately taught to students.
   c. Class discussions on the rationale for different rules should be held.
   d. A large number of rules is preferred to having few rules.

7. Peer norms are most likely to create behavior problems in _____ grades.

   a. preschool
   b. elementary school
   c. middle school
   d. high school

8. The principle of least intervention suggests which of the following sequences of strategies for dealing with misbehavior?

   a. Nonverbal cues, repeated reminders, simple reminders, applying consequences
   b. Simple reminders, nonverbal cues, applying consequences, repeated reminders
   c. Nonverbal cues, simple reminders, repeated reminders, applying consequences
   d. Applying consequences, nonverbal cues, simple reminders, repeated reminders

9. Which type of management intervention is most directly served by giving lively, stimulating lectures?

   a. Verbal cues
   b. Prevention
   c. Praise of others
   d. Nonverbal cues

10. Which of the following is recommended as a first step when students misbehave to gain attention?

a. Ignore the behavior
b. Give the student a time-out
c. Give the student a warning
d. Scold the student briefly

11. Which of the following would be least effective when a student misbehaves to obtain peer approval?

a. Use a group contingency strategy.
b. Give the student a time-out.
c. Discuss the matter with the student privately.
d. Scold the student in front of peers.

12. The first step in setting up a behavior modification plan is to

a. identify target behavior and reinforcer.
b. choose a punisher and criteria for punishment.
c. measure baseline behaviors.
d. observe behavior during program implementation.

13. Which of the following is true regarding effective behavior modification programs?

a. Punishment should be applied in full force, then gradually faded out over time.
b. When the program is working, the frequency of reinforcement should be reduced.
c. Punishment and rewards should be used with fairly equal frequency at the beginning of a program.
d. Punishment should not be used under any circumstances.

14. It is generally recommended that time-outs be

a. fairly brief.
b. used infrequently.
c. applied for misbehavior to gain peer attention.
d. all of the above.

15. A recommended procedure for home-based reinforcement programs is to

a. restrict ratings to the behaviors the individual needs to improve.
b. rate students at the end of every period rather than for the whole day.
c. discourage parents from giving rewards for good behavior.
d. gradually increase the frequency of the home reports as behavior improves.

16. A token reinforcement system is an example of a

    a. group contingency program.
    b. competitive learning structure.
    c. humanistic learning orientation.
    d. whole-class behavior modification system.

17. Which of the following is not an advantage of group contingencies?

    a. They work especially well when the reinforcer for misbehavior is teacher attention.
    b. They work especially well when the reinforcer for misbehavior is peer attention.
    c. They are easier to administer than other behavior modification strategies.
    d. They have produced good results in research studies.

18. The first step in setting up a group contingency program is to

    a. decide which behaviors will be reinforced.
    b. identify the students to whom the program is directed.
    c. identify the group leaders who will help implement the program.
    d. set up a point system.

19. To prevent delinquency, it is considered effective to

    a. use tracking methods of grouping classes.
    b. keep the curriculum the same for college-bound and noncollege-bound students.
    c. suspend students who do not follow rules.
    d. none of the above.

20. Probably the greatest source of influence in maintaining delinquent behavior is

    a. antisocial peer norms.
    b. failure in school.
    c. rejection by parents.
    d. rejection by teachers and school administrators.

APPLICATION: Allocated vs. Engaged Time

How efficiently is instructional time used in classes you attend? Observe two or more instructors from whom you are presently taking courses. Do an informal assessment for each, during different blocks of class time (e.g., 10 minute intervals), of the proportion of engaged time (when students are actively learning) relative to allocated instructional time. Does one instructor typically appear to have the higher ratio? What strategies or characteristics of the instructors observed seem important in accounting for any differences in how efficiently instructional time is used?

APPLICATION: Effective Teacher Strategies

Each of the paragraphs below describes a teacher practicing or demonstrating one of the following:

a. accountability
b. withitness
c. overlapping

Match the appropriate term from the above list to each description. Then explain what the strategy exhibited involves. Which, if any, examples also convey "momentum" and/or "smoothness?" Explain.

A. As Ms. Petrosky writes the day's homework assignment on the chalkboard, she spins around without warning and casts a disapproving eye at Eunice and Ava, who are whispering in the third row. Almost at the same time, she turns toward Johnny and whispers so that only he can hear. "If you didn't do your homework last night, don't use this time to copy Mark's. See me after class to discuss this." Eunice attempts to pass a note to Betty but Ms. Petrosky intercepts it from Betty's grasp. Eunice will join Johnny after school. The rest of the class is cooperative and quiet. They know that Ms. Petrosky is not someone you can easily fool.

B. As Mr. Overton demonstrated proper grips for serving in tennis, he noticed Manuel demonstrating his own grip, a rather obscene one, to Luther. Still talking and moving his arms to demonstrate the serve, Mr. Overton moved quickly over to Manuel, grabbed his hand, positioned his fingers correctly on the racquet, and held his arm and racquet high above his head. "This, class, is the proper grip," Mr. Overton announced. "See how his fingers are positioned around the racquet?" Mr. Overton then gave Manuel's fingers a firm squeeze. Manuel knew what that gesture and the entire episode meant. To the rest of the class, however, it was business as usual. The lesson continued with the backhand grip.

C. Ms. Harper began the biology unit on the brain with a review of yesterday's lesson. She then presented new information on the midbrain, asking "Now what are the two major parts? One is the medulla. The other is the ...?" The class responded "cerebellum." "Good," Ms. Harper said, followed by, "Now which one controls the vital functions such as heart rate and breathing?" The class responded, "medulla." "Good again," she said, "Now here's a question for <u>one</u> of you to answer. What does the cerebellum do? (Waits a few seconds) Mary, how about you?" Mary responds incorrectly. Mrs. Harper says "Think <u>muscles</u> and <u>balance.</u> Now all of you write down four or five things that you would be unable to do if your cerebellum were seriously injured. I'll walk around and see how you're doing." The lesson continued in this way for another fifteen minutes, then it was two o'clock--time to discuss the homework assignments. Ms. Harper announced "Well, all of our brains could use a rest. But to prepare your cerebrums for tonight, let's spend a little time discussing the assignment."

APPLICATION: Classroom Management

Observe one or more classes at the level that you plan to teach. Focus on the teachers' methods of classroom management and results. Would you classify the teachers as successful at classroom management? Explain why or why not in reference to the following questions (whichever ones apply):

1. Do rules appear to be clearly defined?
2. Are rules consistently enforced?
3. Is classwork involving?
4. Are nonverbal cues employed in responding to minor misbehavior?
5. Are good behaviors praised?
6. Are minor misbehaviors ignored as a first response?
7. Are serious misbehaviors, if any, dealt with effectively? How?

APPLICATION: Dealing With Misbehavior

Suppose that you are the regular or substitute teacher in a seventh-grade class. Discuss how you might deal with each of the following behavior problems.

A. While working alone, Alan is usually quiet and serious about the task at hand. But during group instruction he is loud and disruptive. One of his favorite activities is to call out ridiculous answers to questions, which typically provokes laughter from the other students. Just the other day, he volunteered that Bill Cosby was the seventh president of the United States and that Watergate was a famous racehorse. The class seems to anticipate these responses and laughs heartily whether they are funny or not. You have tried to ignore them, but that doesn't seem to have any effect. The main thing is that they are disrupting your lesson, becoming increasingly irritating, and need to be stopped.

B. Maria is a quiet and shy girl around her peers. Around you, however, the story is quite different. She often speaks loudly or even shouts to get your attention. Other times, she completely disobeys instructions, sharpening her pencil when told not to, opening her book during a closed-book exercise, whispering to her neighbor when you are talking. Several times you have punished her by having her stay with you after school. That punishment, however, seems completely ineffective. It has even crossed your mind that she actually seems excited when that punishment is enforced. Something else clearly must be done.

ESSAY/DISCUSSION

1. Describe the characteristics and strategies of a good classroom manager. Can good management styles, in your opinion, be taught or

are they intuitive (a natural skill)?

2. A friend of yours is starting her first day of teaching tomorrow at the high school level. She calls you for advice on getting a good start on course management. You only have a few minutes to talk since you are teaching tomorrow too and need to prepare some materials. What main suggestions would you give?

3. Differentiate between classroom management issues that are prevalent at the elementary school, middle school, and high school levels. At which level, in your opinion, would classroom management be most difficult? Explain.

4. Define and evaluate the "principle of least intervention" as a behavior management philosophy.

5. Describe, using an example behavior problem, the steps involved in using individual behavior modification strategies. Which step(s) do you view as most critical for the strategy to be effective?

6. Suppose that you are using a group contingency system in an eighth-grade class. If any student talks out of turn during independent study, the class will not be allowed to take the field trip to the city power company. Bill, a normally well-behaved boy, encounters difficulty with something and makes a comment without being recognized. Everyone hears it, so you call off the trip. After class, several students complain to you that the punishment just isn't fair. "Everyone was good; Bill made an innocent mistake. Why should we all have to suffer?" Discuss your reactions to this incident. Do you agree with the way the infraction was handled? Are there any changes you would make in similar group contingencies (e.g., for the next field trip) in the future? Explain.

7. Discuss the strategies considered effective in preventing delinquency.

ANSWERS

Matching Warm-ups

Quiz 1

a. 4 (358)
b. 6 (359)
c. 3 (360)
d. 1 (361)
e. 5 (361)
f. 2 (362)

Quiz 2

a. 6 (369)
b. 1 (369)
c. 2 (370)
d. 4 (370)
e. 7 (370)
f. 3 (370)
g. 5 (371)

Key Terms

1.	H (380)	5.	G (378)
2.	D (361)	6.	A (354)
3.	F (374)	7.	B (356)
4.	C (361)	8.	E (362)

Completion Questions

1. allocated (356)
2. engaged (354)
3. momentum (358)
4. accountable (360)
5. alerting (361)
6. withitness (361)
7. overlapping (362)
8. least intervention (369)
9. nonverbal (369)
10. incompatible (370)
11. broken record (370)
12. ignore (374)
13. group contingency (374)
14. target behaviors (376)
15. physical or corporal (379)
16. time-out (378)
17. home-based (380)
18. expulsion (or suspension) (391)
19. whole-class behavior modification (383

Multiple-Choice

1	c (354;357)	11.	d (374)
2.	d (354)	12.	a (376)
3.	a (361)	13.	b (380)
4.	d (361)	14.	d (380)
5.	a (363)	15.	a (380)
6.	d (363)	16.	d (383)
7.	c (366)	17.	a (384)
8.	c (369-371)	18.	a (388)
9.	b (374)	19.	d (390-392)
10.	a (373)	20.	a (389)

12 Exceptional Students

CHAPTER OUTLINE

I. Who is an "Exceptional Student"?
   A. How many students are "exceptional"?

II. Types of Exceptional Students
   A. What's in a label?
   B. Mental exceptionalities
      1. Mental retardation
      2. Characteristics of mentally retarded students
      3. Learning disabilities
      4. Characteristics of learning disabled students
   C. Giftedness
      1. Characteristics of gifted and talented children
      2. Education of the gifted
   D. Teachers on teaching: Teaching gifted children
   E. Serious emotional disturbance
      1. Characteristics of students with emotional disturbances
      2. Aggressive behavior
      3. Withdrawn and immature behavior
      4. Hyperactivity
      5. Other severe emotional disturbances
   F. Behavior disorders
      1. Drug and alcohol abuse
      2. Juvenile delinquency
      3. Family issues: Divorce and death
      4. Child abuse and neglect

G. Communication disorders
   1. Speech disorders
   2. Voice disorders
   3. Speech disorders and the classroom teacher
   4. Language disorders
H. Children with physical problems
   1. Visual impairments
   2. Hearing impairments
   3. Cerebral palsy and seizure disorders
   4. Orthopedic (crippling) handicaps
I. Teachers on teaching: Helping exceptional children

III. Special Education

A. Public Law 94-142
   1. Free and appropriate public education
   2. Least restrictive environment
   3. Individualized Educational Programs (IEPs)
   4. Due process
   5. Evaluation and placement
B. A continuum of special education services
   1. Regular classroom placement
   2. Consultation
   3. Itinerant services
   4. Resource room placement
   5. Special class placement with part-time mainstreaming
   6. Self-contained special education
   7. Special day or residential schools
   8. Homebound and hospital instruction
   9. Other special services
C. Theory into practice: Preparing IEPs
   1. Initial referral
   2. Evaluation/placement team
   3. Preliminary screening
   4. Comprehensive assessment
   5. Writing the IEP
      a. Present performance level
      b. Year's goals
   c. Short-term objectives
      d. Statement of services
      e. Projected initiation date
      f. Evaluation criteria

IV. Mainstreaming
A. Research on mainstreaming
   1. Calhoun and Elliott study
   2. Other research
   3. Effective teaching methods

B. Theory into practice: Adapting instruction
   1. Format adaptations for written assignments
   2. Adaptations in content
   3. Adaptations in modes of communication
C. Computers and the exceptional student
   1. Programs for the handicapped
   2. Using LOGO for independent learning
D. Buddy systems and peer tutoring
   1. Buddy system
   2. Peer tutoring
E. Coordination with special education personnel
   1. What the regular teacher provides
   2. What the special education teacher provides
F. Social integration of exceptional students

Summary/Study Questions/Suggested Readings

CHAPTER OBJECTIVES

1. Define and list characteristics of the major types of exceptionalities.
2. Describe the continuum of educational services available for students with varying degrees of special needs.
3. Define "mainstreaming" and be able to adapt instruction to meet the needs of an exceptional child who spends time in a regular classroom.
4. Describe the procedure for developing Individualized Educational Programs.
5. Describe how to meet the social as well as the academic needs of exceptional children who are mainstreamed.

MATCHING WARM-UPS

Match the numbers of the descriptions on the right to the corresponding items on the left. A given item from the right column may be used more than once or not at all.

Quiz 1: Types of Exceptionalities

_____ a. Mentally retarded		1. Motor impairment caused by brain damage
_____ b. Learning disability		2. Crippling disorder
_____ c. Emotionally disturbed		3. Hyperactivity
_____ d. Communication disorders		4. Attention deficits
_____ e. Cerebral palsy		5. Intellectual impairment
_____ f. Epilepsy		6. Grand mal
_____ g. Orthopedic handicap		7. Stuttering

Quiz 2: Notable Names

_____ a. MA/CA x 100
_____ b. Verbal and performance IQ
_____ c. First IQ test
_____ d. Study of gifted
_____ e. Intelligence, wisdom, and creativity
_____ f. WISC-R

1. Sternberg
2. Wechsler
3. Binet
4. Terman

KEY TERMS

Fill in the blanks below with the letters identifying the following concepts. Each concept is used one time only.

A. Exceptionality
B. Intelligence quotient
C. Normal curve
D. Mental retardation
E. Educable mentally retarded
F. Trainable mentally retarded
G. Learning disability
H. Attention deficit
I. Emotionally disturbed
J. Hyperactivity
K. Speech disorders
L. Cerebral palsy
M. Special education
N. Public Law 94-142
O. Mainstreaming
P. Individualized Education Program

1. A mental, emotional, or physical condition that creates special educational needs represents _____.

2. A disorder in which motor functioning is impaired by brain damage is _____.

3. Articulation or voice problems that frequently occur in elementary school grades are symptomatic of _____.

4. The placement of handicapped individuals with nonhandicapped peers is called _____.

5. Subaverage intellectual functioning and poor adaptive skills are generally labeled as _____.

6. Children demonstrating _____ tend to be restless, are unable to sit still or concentrate, and have short attention spans.

7. A measurement introduced by Binet to determine mental abilities is the _____.

8. A bell-shaped distribution in which most scores fall near the center is called the _____.

9. Programs provided for handicapped children as a substitute for or addition to regular programs are part of what is generally called _____.

10. Children who are unable to learn for reasons other than intellectual, sensory, or health factors are classified as _____.

11. The inability to concentrate for a sustained period of time is called a(n)_____.

12. The rights of handicapped children and the services they must receive are specified in _____.

13. For each handicapped student, a(n) _____ must be prepared to describe his/her specific problems and detail the course of action to remedy those problems.

14. A category of mental retardation that encompasses mild handicaps is _____.

15. A category of mental retardation that encompasses moderate handicaps is _____.

16. A disorder that impedes the academic progress of students who often have normal to superior intellectual abilities is a(n) _____.

COMPLETION QUESTIONS

1. The type of exceptionality that has shown the largest increase over the past decade is _____.

2. The intelligence quotient, as created by Binet, was computed by dividing _____ by _____.

3. Intelligence and many other human traits are distributed as a(n) _____.

4. The average IQ is _____.

5. Educational programs for individuals classified as _____ mentally retarded emphasize "self-help" and living skills," whereas those for individuals classified as _____ mentally retarded focus on basic academic skills.

6. A student who is not mentally retarded, emotionally disturbed, or environmentally disadvantaged is falling significantly behind his classmates in learning to read. This disorder would most likely be classified as a _____.

7. The inability to concentrate or focus on tasks for long periods of time is called an _____.

8. Terman's classic research involved a long-term study of the lives of individuals identified as _____.

9. Differences of opinion regarding teaching of the gifted concern whether to emphasize acceleration or _____.

10. Children classified as _____ exhibit problems with learning, interpersonal relationships, and controlling of feelings and behavior.

11. Drugs such as Ritalin or Dexedrine are often prescribed to control the behavior pattern called _____.

12. The most common type of speech disorder consists of _____ problems.

13. A motor impairment caused by damage to the brain is _____.

14. A major seizure characterized by loss of consciousness, rigidity, and shaking is called a _____.

15. The federal law requiring provision of special education services to eligible students is _____.

16. Handicapped students are placed with nonhandicapped students as much as possible under _____ practices.

17. Special education teachers in consultation with other members of a team prepare an _____ for each handicapped student to guide the services the student will receive.

18. The least restrictive of all placements is to assign the handicapped student to a _____.

19. A computer language that has been used successfully to involve handicapped children in active learning is _____.

20. Handicapped students are paired with nonhandicapped students who help them with classroom activities under the _____ system.

MULTIPLE-CHOICE

Select the best answer for each of the following items.

1. Which of the following types of handicaps is most common for students served today in educational programs?

   a. Speech impaired
   b. Emotionally disturbed
   c. Learning disabled
   d. Orthopedically handicapped

2. Which of the following is <u>not</u> a major category of exceptionality?

   a. Mental
   b. Speech or language
   c. Social
   d. Emotional

3. Using Binet's system, a six-year-old student with a mental age of 9 would have an IQ of

   a. 67
   b. 100
   c. 120
   d. 150

4. Given the properties of the IQ distribution, which of the following IQ scores would be <u>most</u> common?

   a. 90
   b. 105
   c. 120
   d. 122

5. Which of the following is <u>not</u> one of the three types of intellectual abilities hypothesized by Sternberg?

   a. Logic
   b. Intelligence
   c. Wisdom
   d. Creativity

6. Trainable mental retardation implies

   a. severe retardation.
   b. the capability of learning academic skills up to the sixth grade.
   c. mild retardation.
   d. none of the above.

7. An individual with a learning disability is likely to

   a. have an attention deficit.
   b. be mentally retarded.
   c. come from a disadvantaged home environment.
   d. be emotionally disturbed.

8. Terman's classic study found that gifted children tend to be

   a. socially inept.
   b. less athletic than their peers.
   c. better adjusted as adults than their peers.
   d. teachers' pets.

9. Research on the effects of gifted programs on achievement has provided

   a. more support for enrichment programs than for acceleration programs.
   b. more support for acceleration programs than for enrichment programs.
   c. no indication that either acceleration or enrichment is effective.
   d. equal support for both acceleration and enrichment programs.

10. A problem with using drugs to treat hyperactivity is

   a. chemical dependency often occurs.
   b. costs are prohibitive for the typical family.
   c. proper behavioral control is not taught.
   d. their lack of effectiveness in making children more manageable.

11. Which of the following affects girls to almost the same extent as it does boys?

   a. Learning disabilities
   b. Occasional drug or alcohol use
   c. Hyperactivity
   d. Heavy drug or alcohol use

12. When teachers suspect child abuse, they

   a. should keep those suspicions to themselves to avoid defamation of character suits by parents.
   b. have an ethical obligation to report it.
   c. should contact the parents to discuss the problem.
   d. none of the above.

13. Which of the following is recommended for teachers when interacting with students having speech disorders?

   a. Refrain from correcting the student in class
   b. Allow others to finish the student's sentences when he/she is having trouble
   c. Put the student in situations involving quick verbal responses
   d. Have the student orally respond in class only when absolutely necessary.

14. Cerebral palsy is most likely to be associated with

   a. visual problems.
   b. motor problems.
   c. mental retardation.
   d. seizures.

15. IEP stands for

   a. Innovative Educational Plan.
   b. Individualized Environmental Program.
   c. Integrated Environmental Placement.
   d. Individualized Educational Program.

16. Which of the following types of special educational services is the <u>least</u> restrictive?

   a. Resource room placement
   b. Homebound instruction
   c. Self-contained special education
   d. Special class placement with part-time mainstreaming

17. An IEP is usually written by

   a. the parents and the regular teacher.
   b. the school principal.
   c. the special education teacher and the regular teacher.
   d. an evaluation placement team and the special education teacher.

18. Results of the Calhoun and Elliott (1977) study were

   a. damaging to the idea of least restrictive placements.
   b. inconclusive regarding special education placements.
   c. supportive of within-class ability grouping.
   d. supportive of mainstreaming.

19. An advantage of using Logo with handicapped children is

   a. helping them to read.
   b. helping them select and appropriately combine parts of a sentence.
   c. allowing them to experiment with picture-drawing, problem-solving, and programming.
   d. teaching them to write creatively without the fear of making errors.

20. In a "buddy system" a handicapped student works cooperatively with

a. another handicapped student.
b. a nonhandicapped student.
c. the regular classroom teacher.
d. an adult volunteer from the community.

APPLICATION: Least Restrictive Environment

Suppose that you are selected to serve on a special panel that is assigned the task of recommending services for handicapped students at your neighborhood middle school. Listed below are various options. Rank them in order of restrictiveness, starting with the least restrictive. Briefly indicate for each the type of student most likely to need that service.

A. There is a separate classroom in the school that is supervised by a special education teacher. There is space available for additional children to remain full-time in that class.

B. There is a resource room in the school that is supervised by a trained resource teacher. There is space available for additional students to spend time there, according to needs.

C. There are consultants available to suggest materials and strategies for regular teachers to use in helping handicapped students.

D. There is a special day school in the community that handicapped children can attend full-time.

E. There is a separate classroom in the school that is supervised by a special education teacher. Space is available for additional students to work there part of the day when they are not in their regular class.

F. Itinerant teachers are available in the district who can provide special services to handicapped students for a few hours each week.

APPLICATION: Field Experience in Special Education Services

Visit school classes attended by the age groups you plan to teach. Interview the teachers with regard to the following:

A. How frequently are handicapped students placed in their classes?

B. What types of handicapping conditions have been represented?

C. What types of special teaching methods or adaptations have they tried?

D. Have any types of handicaps been more difficult to accommodate than others?

E. Is there any type of teacher training, not provided by their college programs, that they feel would be helpful to them in working with handicapped students?

APPLICATION: Adapting Instruction

Adapting instruction to exceptional students requires knowing the individual students, not just their condition. Nonetheless, information about the condition can still be quite valuable in devising a preliminary plan. Read each of the descriptions below and describe what types of special adaptations might be considered for such preliminary plans.

A. Margaret is a sixth-grader who will be in your social studies class. She is fourteen years old (about three years older than the sixth-grade norm), has an IQ of 75, and is classified as educable mentally retarded. Although she can do sixth-grade work in most subjects, it is realistic to expect her to trail behind other students in speed and level of performance.

B. Roberto, who will be in your eighth-grade math class, has an IQ of 175 and a superior academic record in all subjects. Last year in math class, he "placed out" on seventh-, eighth-, and ninth-grade materials, and ended up the year successfully completing a college algebra text.

C. Stephen, an above average eight-year-old, is in your third-grade class. He has been described by other teachers as hyperactive, as evidenced by his short attention span, need to move (fidget) almost constantly, and general impulsiveness. He takes Ritlin each day, and it helps somewhat. However, you are not completely satisfied with the results.

D. Marsha, an otherwise normal (average) student in your high school English class, has a vision problem that makes it difficult for her to focus on close stimuli, such as small print and small objects. She does not have a problem, however, focusing on distant stimuli such as you or the blackboard. She tells you her main worry is reading the questions on tests.

E. Catherine is a slightly below average student in your high school chemistry class. She is conscientious and is capable of doing the work. However, she has a moderate hearing problem in which she can perceive about 40 decibels with a hearing aid. You suspect that she is able to follow most but not all of typical class discussion.

F. George is an above average student in your seventh-grade social studies class. He suffers from epilepsy and is prone to having grand mal seizures (he had three in school last year).

ESSAY/DISCUSSION

1. Discuss what is meant by "exceptionality." Explain how that label can encompass such extremes as a mentally retarded adolescent functioning at the first-grade level and a gifted elementary school child who is able to master college-level materials?

2. Discuss how IQ scores are distributed and what they imply about an individual. What, in your opinion, are the advantages and disadvantages of IQ testing? Would our educational system be better off if IQ testing were completely abolished? Explain.

3. Describe the developmental characteristics and learning potential of children classified as mildly, moderately, and severely retarded.

4. Explain how "learning disability" differs from "mental retardation."

5. Define mainstreaming and evaluate, based on your feelings, its implications for handicapped students, nonhandicapped students, and regular classroom teachers.

6. Should teachers be held legally responsible for reporting suspected incidents of child abuse or neglect? Explain your rationale.

7. Discuss the problem of socially integrating exceptional students in regular classrooms. What can teachers do to facilitate that process?

ANSWERS

Matching Warm-Ups

Quiz 1

a. 5 (400)
b. 4 (402)
c. 3 (407)
d. 7 (413)
e. 1 (416)
f. 6 (417)
g. 2 (420)

Quiz 2

a. 3 (398)
b. 2 (399)
c. 3 (398)
d. 4 (404)
e. 1 (399)
f. 2 (399)

Key Terms

1. A (396)
2. L (416)
3. K (412)
4. O (421)
5. D (399)
6. J (409)
7. B (398)
8. C (398)
9. M (420)
10. I (407)
11. H (403)
12. N (420)
13. P (421)
14. E (400)
15. F (400)
16. G (402)

Completion Questions

1. learning disabilities (397)
2. mental age; chronological age (398)
3. normal curve (398)
4. 100 (399)
5. trainable; educable (400)
6. learning disability (402-403)
7. attention deficit (403)
8. gifted (404)
9. enrichment (406)
10. emotionally disturbed (407)
11. hyperactivity (409)
12. articulation (412)
13. cerebral palsy (416)
14. grand mal (417)
15. PL 94-142 (420)
16. mainstreaming (421)
17. Individualized Education Program (421)
18. regular class (423)
19. Logo (434)
20. buddy (434)

Multiple-Choice

1.	c (397)	11.	b (410)
2.	c (396)	12.	b (411)
3.	d (398)	13.	a (413)
4.	b (399)	14.	b (416)
5.	a (399)	15.	d (421)
6.	d (400)	16.	d (422-425)
7.	a (403)	17.	c (427)
8.	c (404)	18.	d (429)
9.	b (406)	19.	c (434)
10.	c (410)	20.	b (434)

Application: Least Restrictive Environment

Correct order, from least to most restrictive, is:

C, F, B, E, A, D

13 Social Class, Ethnicity, and Gender

CHAPTER OUTLINE

I. Cultural Differences

II. Social Class
- A. Schools as middle-class institutions
  1. Individuality
  2. Future time orientation
  3. Implications for teachers
- B. Compensatory education
  1. Chapter I program
  2. Research on compensatory education

III. Ethnicity and Race
- A. Racial and ethnic composition of the United States
  1. Population breakdowns
  2. Academic achievement of minority students
- B. Desegregation
  1. Brown vs. Board of Education case
  2. Effects of desegregation on achievement
- C. Theory into practice: Teaching in desegregated schools
  1. Fairness
  2. Balance
  3. Avoiding resegregation
  4. Intergroup relations

IV. Language Minorities
- A. Bilingual education
  1. Types of programs
  2. Research on bilingual education

B. Theory into practice: Teaching in the culturally diverse classroom

V. Gender Differences

A. Actual vs. learned gender differences
   1. Females exhibit greater verbal aptitude than males
   2. Males exceed females in visual-spatial aptitude
   3. Males exceed females in mathematical aptitude
   4. Males are more aggressive than females both physically and verbally

B. Gender differences in early socialization

C. Gender differences and the school

D. Teachers on teaching: Social-class, ethnic, and gender differences

E. Gender differences in achievement

F. Social-class and sex-role differences

G. Theory into practice: Avoiding gender bias in teaching
   1. Avoiding stereotypes
   2. Promoting integration
   3. Equal treatment of girls and boys

Summary/Study Questions/Suggested Readings

CHAPTER OBJECTIVES

1. List ways in which social class affects upbringing and achievement.
2. List middle-class values that are reflected in educational practices.
3. Describe the role of the federal government in helping students from disadvantaged backgrounds.
4. Define "ethnic group," and contrast it to "social class."
5. Understand the issues that are of special importance to teachers in desegregated schools and in schools where some students speak little or no English.
6. Describe some gender differences that are biologically based and some that are learned, and understand how to avoid reinforcing sex roles.

MATCHING WARM-UP

Match the numbers of the descriptions on the right to the corresponding items on the left. A given item from the right column may be used more than once or not at all.

Gender Differences (Maccoby & Jacklin, 1974)

_____ a. Aggression
_____ b. Mathematical aptitude
_____ c. Verbal aptitude
_____ d. Social orientation
_____ e. Suggestibility
_____ f. Visual-spatial aptitude
_____ g. Self-esteem
_____ h. Rote memory

1. Males exceed females
2. Females exceed males
3. No gender differences

KEY TERMS

Fill in the blanks below with the letters identifying the following concepts. Each concept is used one time only.

A. Culture
B. Socioeconomic status
C. Compensatory education
D. Chapter I
E. Ethnic group
F. Desegregation
G. Bilingual education

1. A group of people who share race, religion, and/or place of origin comprise a(n) _____.

2. Programs specifically designed to supplement the education of students from disadvantaged backgrounds are called _____ programs.

3. A group's prestige and income level is represented by their _____.

4. A specific federal program that gives schools money to improve educational services for disadvantaged students is _____.

5. Students having limited proficiency in English are taught part of the time in their own language in _____ programs.

6. The language, attitudes, and ways of behaving characteristic of a group of people comprise the _____ of that group.

7. The placement of minority students in schools attended by white students is the goal of _____.

COMPLETION QUESTIONS

1. Differences in the languages, food preferences, values, and behaviors of various groups of people make up their _____.

2. Individuals who have high incomes and many years of education are assessed as having high _____.

3. Head Start and Follow-Through are examples of _____ programs.

4. Funds from the _____ program must be used to "supplement, not supplant" local efforts to educate disadvantaged students.

5. The questionable procedure of removing disadvantaged students from regular classes to give them special help takes place in _____ programs.

6. A group of people who share a sense of identity, usually because of race, origin, or religion, comprise an _____.

7. The largest racial and ethnic group within the United States is formed by _____.

8. Two ethnic groups that have recently gained more rapidly than whites on the SATs are black and _____ students.

9. The landmark case in which the Supreme Court abolished legal segregation is _____.

10. Programs that teach subjects in the native languages of students who have limited English proficiency are referred to as _____ education programs.

11. The language most often used in special programs as an alternative to English is _____.

12. When a language-minority student has a comprehension problem, a _____ system can be tried by pairing the student with one who can speak both the minority language and English.

13. Females have been found to have higher _____ aptitude than males.

14. Males have been found to exceed females in both _____ aptitude and _____ aptitude.

15. A personality characteristic exhibited more by males than females and believed to be biologically influenced is _____.

16. Teachers promote sexual _____ by making comments such as "Girls are neat," "Boys are strong," etc.

MULTIPLE-CHOICE

Select the best answer for each of the following items.

1. Which of the following is NOT considered part of an individual's socioeconomic status?

    a. Income
    b. IQ
    c. Education
    d. Prestige in society

2. The culture of most schools in the United States tends to reflect

   a. the values of the majority of students who attend.
   b. lower-class values.
   c. upper-class values.
   d. middle-class values.

3. In studies of child-rearing practices of lower- and middle-class mothers, the lower-class mothers

   a. had higher expectations for their children.
   b. used more expressive language.
   c. gave clearer directions.
   d. none of the above.

4. SES stands for

   a. systematized educational support.
   b. socioeconomic status.
   c. social-educational systems.
   d. situational environmental scale.

5. In Heyns' study, achievement by lower-class and middle-class students during the school year and summer was analyzed. Results implied that

   a. lower-class students have inferior abilities.
   b. lower-class students receive less cognitive stimulation at home.
   c. social class has no influence on school achievement.
   d. students learn best from teachers of the same social class.

6. A child from a lower-class background is likely to perform better when

   a. rewards are immediate.
   b. the goal structure is competitive.
   c. there is much individual freedom in learning.
   d. the teacher uses a permissive management orientation.

7. The purpose of Chapter I programs is to

   a. promote use of bilingual education with language minority students.
   b. use government money to improve home and neighborhood environments.
   c. provide grants for qualified disadvantaged students to attend college.
   d. provide money to schools for special services to disadvantaged students.

8. The main problem that appears to occur with "pull out" programs is

   a. the large class sizes that result in the Chapter I classes.
   b. negative attitudes by students who are not selected for Chapter I programs.
   c. lack of communication between the regular teacher and the Chapter I teacher.
   d. lack of space in school buildings to accommodate Chapter I classes.

9. Next to blacks, the minority group with the greatest representation in the United States population is

   a. Hispanic.
   b. Chinese.
   c. Japanese.
   d. American Indian.

10. Comparisons between academic achievement of Anglo-Americans and minorities consisting of Hispanics and blacks show

   a. no significant difference in either English or math.
   b. significantly lower minority scores in both English and math.
   c. similar scores in math, but a minority disadvantage in English.
   d. similar scores in English, but a minority disadvantage in math.

11. Recent findings regarding Scholastic Achievement Test (SAT) scores of different ethnic groups show that

   a. differences favoring whites over black students have diminished during the past few years.
   b. white students are gaining more rapidly than black and Chicano students.
   c. Chicano students have just about reached the level of white students.
   d. the highest scores of all groups are being obtained by American Indian students.

12. A direct product of the Brown vs. Board of Education case was

   a. Title I.
   b. desegregation.
   c. bilingual education.
   d. Chapter I.

13. Which of the following is true about language minority students in the United States?

   a. Their representation in the population is decreasing.
   b. They tend to excel in athletic abilities.
   c. They tend to achieve below grade level in most subjects.
   d. All of the above.

14. Research supports the overall conclusion that school desegregation has

   a. been more detrimental than beneficial to minority students.
   b. surpassed its expectations by providing large minority achievement gains.
   c. produced small, but positive achievement gains for minorities.
   d. consistently raised the quality of education received by minorities.

15. Which of the following strategies is <u>not</u> recommended for teaching in culturally diverse classrooms?

   a. Promoting competition through games and learning activities
   b. Using a "buddy" system
   c. Discussing traditions of different cultures
   d. Encouraging activities that involve interactions with peers

16. The consensus of researchers is that sex differences are mostly a product of

   a. genetic factors.
   b. inherent biological differences.
   c. socialization experiences.
   d. trends depicted in radio and television.

17. Which of the following statements is true?

   a. Females are more social than males.
   b. Females are more suggestible than males.
   c. Males exceed females in visual-spatial aptitude.
   d. All of the above.

18. In interacting with male and female students, teachers tend to

   a. reward creative behavior of females more than males.
   b. tolerate aggressive behavior less for females than for males.
   c. punish females in general more than males.
   d. interact less with males than with females in such areas as approval and instruction giving.

19. Studies of achievement and ability differences between the sexes indicate that

    a. girls have an initial academic advantage over boys in elementary school.
    b. mathematical differences favoring males tend to decrease in the higher grades.
    c. males score higher in IQ than females.
    d. there is more variability in ability among females than among males.

20. A set of middle-class and lower-class parents each have a daughter who wants to play football. Which of the following outcomes seems most probable?

    a. Both sets of parents will be supportive.
    b. The middle-class parents will be less supportive than the lower-class parents.
    c. The lower-class parents will be less supportive than the middle-class parents.
    d. All seem equally likely to occur.

<u>APPLICATION:</u> Teaching in Culturally Diverse Classrooms

The paragraphs below describe a teaching situation involving culturally diverse classrooms. Describe what special strategy or adjustments you might use in dealing with each.

A. You are teaching a sixth-grade class comprised of 20 students in a lower-class to middle-class neighborhood. Of the 20 students, 8 are black and 12 are white. You notice that during free time in class and on the playground, student groupings and interactions closely follow racial lines: blacks interact with blacks and whites with whites.

B. You are teaching ninth-grade social studies in a middle-class urban middle school. The class consists of black and Anglo-American students. There are, however, several Oriental students and one Hispanic student. The latter individual speaks Spanish as his primary language and is very poor in comprehending and speaking English. Your suspicion is that this student follows very little of the lectures you present and has poor comprehension of reading assignments completed in restricted time periods.

C. You are teaching seventh-grade math to students living in an extremely poor neighborhood. Socioeconomic status of nearly all of the families concerned is below the poverty line. Many of the students seem willing to learn, but you are having problems motivating them using some of the methods you developed while student teaching in an upper-middle-class suburban school.

D. In your tenth-grade physical education class at a middle-class school, there are 20 white students and only one black student. You observe that the black student is excluded by the others, being picked close to last in team competitions and given little attention by the others. This student appears to be better than average at sports, yet is demonstrating little improvement or enthusiasm for participating.

APPLICATION: Field Experience in Observing Cultural and Ethnic Differences

Visit one or more classes in the subject, grade level, and type of school (city, suburban, etc.) corresponding with your teaching interests. Note the racial and/or ethnic make-up of the class. Observe students' interactions with each other and with the teacher. Does race (ethnic group) appear to influence these interactions (who talks with whom, what is said, etc.)? Ask the teacher(s), where appropriate, to comment on the following: (1) Are there racial (ethnic) problems or tensions in the class? (2) Are special techniques needed to teach a culturally diverse class? If so what? (3) What special techniques, if any, are needed to teach disadvantaged students? (4) What provisions are made for language minority students?

APPLICATION: Evaluating Teaching Practices

The following sections briefly describe hypothetical practices used by teachers in dealing with social class, ethnic, or gender differences. Evaluate each based on your feelings about its effectiveness. Explain the rationale for your evaluation.

A. The families sending their children to a certain school are varied in socioeconomic status. Between-class ability grouping is used in many grades to accommodate individual differences.

B. Ms. Henderson has several language minority students in her fourth-grade class. She pairs each with a bilingual student fluent in both English and the partner's primary language.

C. Mr. Ortez, who has many economically disadvantaged children in his fourth-grade class, emphasizes individualized work over cooperative activities.

D. Ms. Bealer is a physical education teacher at an elementary school attended by 40% black and 60% Anglo-American students. She does not allow the students to choose sides in competitive games to prevent the possibility of team selection occurring along racial lines.

E. Ms. Dudley teaches junior-high algebra in a school located in a poor neighborhood. She provides many incentives for satisfactory completion of homework, but delays giving the rewards (for example, a field trip or free time) until the end of the term to avoid "spoiling" the students.

F. Ms. Costner, who teaches a culturally mixed eighth-grade music class of Anglo-Americans, blacks, Hispanics, and Oriental children, tries to select music that is "culture-free" and does not favor one group's values or preferences over another's. She fears that culturally-oriented selections will create negative feelings among the other groups.

G. Ms. James encourages girls and boys in her first-grade class to explore all toys and games, such as dolls, baseballs, tools, etc., not just certain types.

ESSAY/DISCUSSION

1. Define what is meant by social class, and describe its probable implications for school achievement and motivation. Differentiate between teaching strategies that appear best suited for lower-class and middle-class students.

2. Head Start and similar programs are designed to provide supplemental education to help children from disadvantaged homes. Discuss your position regarding the value of such programs. Specifically, can they make a difference? Are the differences, if any, likely to be lasting? What changes would you make if you were designing or administering such programs.

3. An ongoing debate concerns whether IQ differences between ethnic groups are more attributable to heredity or to environment. Regardless of the position you may favor, which interpretation has the greater implications for teachers and the methods they use?

4. Discuss the arguments for and against bilingual education. Which position do you personally support? Explain.

5. Summarize the results of studies comparing males and females on aptitude and personality variables. Based on these outcomes, is there sufficient reason to treat males and females differently in planning and delivering educational activities? Explain.

ANSWERS

Matching Warm-Up

a.	1 (456)	e.	3 (456)
b.	1 (456)	f.	1 (456)
c.	2 (456)	g.	3 (456)
d.	3 (456)	h.	3 (456)

Key Terms

1. E (447)
2. C (445)
3. B (442)
4. D (445)
5. G (453)
6. A (441)
7. F (449)

Completion Questions

1. cultures (441)
2. socioeconomic status (442)
3. compensatory education (445)
4. Chapter I (445)
5. pull-out (445)
6. ethnic group (447)
7. non-Hispanic whites (447)
8. Chicano (448)
9. Brown vs. Board of Educ. (449)
10. bilingual (453)
11. Spanish (453)
12. buddy (454)
13. verbal (456)
14. mathematical; visual-spatial (456)
15. aggression (456)
16. stereotypes (461)

Multiple-Choice

1. b (442)
2. d (443)
3. d (442)
4. b (442)
5. b (443)
6. a (444)
7. d (445)
8. c (445)
9. a (447)
10. b (448)
11. a (448)
12. b (449)
13. c (452)
14. c (450)
15. a (455)
16. c (455)
17. c (456)
18. b (459)
19. a (460)
20. c (460-461)

14 Student Evaluation: Tests and Grades

CHAPTER OUTLINE

I. Student Evaluation

II. Why Do We Evaluate?
  A. Evaluation as incentives
    1. Important evaluations
    2. Soundly based evaluations
    3. Consistent standards
    4. Reliable interpretations of evaluations
    5. Frequent evaluations
    6. Challenging evaluations
  B. Informational value of evaluations
    1. Evaluations as feedback to students
    2. Evaluations as feedback to teachers
    3. Evaluations as information to parents
    4. Evaluations as information for selection
  C. Teachers on teaching: Tests and their uses

III. Evaluation Strategies
  A. Formative versus summative evaluation
    1. Formative asks "how are we doing?"
    2. Summative asks "how did we do?"
  B. Norm-referenced versus criterion-referenced evaluation
    1. Norm-referenced compares students to others
    2. Criterion-referenced assesses mastery of specific skills
  C. Matching strategies with goals
    1. Incentive/feedback/evaluation
    2. Comparative evaluations

IV. Achievement Tests
   A. Basic principles of achievement testing
      1. Measure clearly defined objectives
      2. Measure a representative sample of learning tasks
      3. Include appropriate types of test items
      4. Should fit uses of results
      5. Should be as reliable as possible
      6. Should improve learning
   B. Tables of specifications
   C. Theory into practice: Writing test items
      1. Multiple-choice items
      2. True-false items
      3. Fill-in-the-blank items
      4. Matching items
      5. Short essay items
      6. Evaluating short essay items
      7. Problem-solving items
      8. Evaluating problem solving
         a. Partial credit
         b. Congruence between test items and instructional objectives
   D. Teachers on teaching: Designing tests

V. Grading and Evaluating
   A. Grading criteria
   B. Assigning letter grades
      1. Absolute grading standards
      2. Relative grading standards
      3. Other approaches to grading
   C. Teachers on teaching: Grading
   D. Report card grades

Summary/Study Questions/Suggested Readings

CHAPTER OBJECTIVES

1. List several reasons for evaluating students.
2. Describe purposes served by evaluating students (1) during instruction versus after instruction, and (2) on the basis of mastery of specific skills and knowledge versus performance relative to other students.
3. Write a table of specifications for a test that links assessment to instructional objectives and lesson content.
4. Develop tests that accurately measure skills and knowledge using appropriate types of questions.
5. Assign letter grades that represent levels of student performance fairly.

MATCHING WARM-UPS

Match the numbers of the descriptions on the right to the corresponding items on the left. A given item from the right column may be used more than once or not at all.

Quiz 1: Approaches to Achievement Testing

_____ a. Formative evaluation emphasis
_____ b. Broad in coverage
_____ c. Mastery testing
_____ d. Absolute standards
_____ e. Maximum item discrimination

1. Norm-referenced
2. Criterion-referenced

Quiz 2: Types of Tests

_____ a. Probably least preferred
_____ b. Tests higher-level reasoning
_____ c. Test-wiseness = Ø
_____ d. Lists should be short
_____ e. Very useful and flexible

1. Multiple-choice
2. True-false
3. Fill-in-the-blank
4. Matching items
5. Short essay

Quiz 3: Grading Methods

_____ a. Number of units completed
_____ b. Retest if below standard
_____ c. Class ranking
_____ d. Preestablished criteria

1. Absolute
2. Relative
3. Mastery
4. Continuous progress

KEY TERMS

Fill in the blanks below with the letters identifying the following concepts. Each concept is used one time only.

A. Student evaluation
B. Formative evaluations
C. Summative evaluations
D. Norm-referenced evaluations
E. Criterion-referenced evaluations
F. Reliability
G. Table of specifications
H. Distractors
I. Evaluative descriptors
J. Absolute grading standards
K. Relative grading
L. Mastery grading
M. Continuous progress grading

1. Teachers who determine grades on the basis of the number of units students complete are using _____.

2. When teachers grade "on the curve," they are using _____.

3. The consistency of scores from one testing to the next is defined as test _____.

4. Written or oral critiques of aspects of responses to examination questions are _____.

5. Pre-established percentage scores are used as criteria for given grades in _____.

6. Tests that determine how well students have mastered specific skills or areas of knowledge represent _____.

7. Tests given to determine strengths and weaknesses in learning while a unit is being taught represent _____.

8. A device for allocating test items among important topics and objectives is a(n) _____.

9. A grading system that bases a student's grade according to whether a standard criterion is reached the first time is _____.

10. Tests that compare the performance of one student against the performances of others represent _____.

11. Tests given to determine student knowledge or skills at the end of a unit represent _____.

12. The incorrect alternative answers to a multiple-choice question are called _____.

13. Formal assessment of student performance using tests, written reports, and grades is generally referred to as _____.

<u>COMPLETION QUESTIONS</u>

1. An important advantage of student evaluation is providing _____ to students and teachers regarding the effectiveness of their performances.

2. Evaluation is useful in _____ decisions by identifying which students are more or less likely than others to succeed in given fields or programs.

3. The type of evaluation used to determine how students are doing <u>while</u> learning is _____.

4. The type of evaluation used to determine how students performed at the completion of a lesson is _____.

5. Standardized tests which evaluate examinees in comparison to others are a form of _____ evaluation.

6. Tests that determine whether students can perform at levels specified by absolute standards are _____ tests.

7. Tests used for _____ purposes should be given more frequently than tests given for comparative purposes.

8. When individual students' scores on a test are consistent from one test administration to the next, the test is said to be _____.

9. A device used to guide test development by listing instructional objectives and expected levels of understanding is a _____.

10. The type of test item most susceptible to measurement error caused by guessing is the _____ item.

11. The items in this section are examples of _____ items.

12. A type of item that allows students to express themselves in their own words, but limits the length of the response is the _____ item.

13. Many measurement specialists consider _____ items to be the most useful and flexible of all item types.

14. A type of item that allows the teacher to evaluate how the student sequenced and organized steps on a complex task, in addition to the correctness of the final answer is the _____ item.

15. Mr. Byers grades students such that the top 5 (out of 20) receive A's, the next 5 receive B's, and so on. He is using _____ grading standards.

16. Mrs. Sellers grades students such that 95 to 100 = A, 85 to 94 = B, etc. She is using _____ grading standards.

17. In Mr. Rosen's chemistry laboratory class, students who complete 10 experiments receive an A, 8 experiments B, 6 experiments C, and 4 experiments D. He is using _____ grading.

MULTIPLE-CHOICE

Select the best answer for each of the following items.

1. Your text indicates that evaluations should be "soundly based." This means that

   a. standardized tests are emphasized over teacher-made tests.
   b. students feel that evaluations are valid measures of their performance.
   c. evaluations are assigned high importance by parents, teachers, and students.
   d. teacher-made tests use a variety of item types rather than one type exclusively.

2. School evaluations become <u>less</u> effective when

   a. attaining success is challenging for all students.
   b. tests are given infrequently rather than often.
   c. criteria are consistent for all students.
   d. parents take an active interest in them.

3. Which of the following is the most typical function of summative evaluations?

   a. Comparison of students
   b. Diagnosis
   c. Devising lesson plans
   d. Revising ability group tracks

4. The major emphasis of criterion-referenced tests is

   a. student selection.
   b. assessing performances over a broad area content domain.
   c. providing information to support summative evaluation.
   d. determining what tasks students can perform.

5. Based on the expectancy theory of motivation, which of the following practices would be recommended?

   a. Make success desirable but challenging
   b. Make tests easy for students, especially at the beginning of the year
   c. Use pass-fail systems in honors classes
   d. Drop the lowest score when final grades are based on more than three tests

6. Typically, formative evaluations are also

   a. summative evaluations.
   b. norm-referenced tests.
   c. criterion-referenced tests.
   d. final examinations.

7. Which of the following is the least appropriate use of achievement tests?

   a. Predicting student performance in a course of study
   b. Determining student aptitude for a subject
   c. Serving as a formative test of student progress
   d. Serving as a summative test of student learning

8. Test reliability is increased by

   a. decreasing test length.
   b. increasing test length.
   c. using very difficult items that few students get right.
   d. using very easy items that few students miss.

9. Compared to multiple-choice items, true-false items are

   a. more valid for low-achieving students.
   b. more difficult to construct.
   c. more susceptible to influences of random guessing.
   d. all of the above.

10. A procedure that is <u>not</u> recommended in writing multiple-choice items is

   a. listing choices vertically rather than horizontally.
   b. making the correct choice approximately the same length as the distractors.
   c. selecting positions of correct answers on a random basis.
   d. including at least one distractor that is clearly implausible.

11. For which type of test would the teacher be most likely to use evaluative descriptors?

   a. True-false
   b. Multiple-choice
   c. Problem solving
   d. Fill-in-the blank

12. A serious limitation of essay tests is that they

   a. encourage poor study habits.
   b. require too much time to construct.
   c. are difficult to score reliably.
   d. all of the above.

13. A recommended procedure for matching tests is to

   a. direct them toward testing higher levels of learning.
   b. keep the A and B lists the exact same length.
   c. make the list at least 8-16 items in length.
   d. none of the above.

14. Comparisons between graded and pass-fail systems show

   a. higher performances under pass-fail systems.
   b. higher performances under graded systems.
   c. no differences between them in student performance.
   d. higher performances for high-achievers under graded systems and higher performance for low-achievers under non-graded systems.

15. Ms. Larsen uses a relative grading system. The first student whose test she grades earns a score of 88% correct. What can be concluded about that student's letter grade?

   a. It is definitely an A.
   b. It is definitely a B.
   c. It is definitely not a C.
   d. Nothing can be concluded at this point.

16. Mr. Lynfield uses a continuous progress grading system. His concern in assigning course grades will be

   a. the students' average scores.
   b. the number of units the students complete.
   c. whether the students reach mastery on a final exam.
   d. how the students perform relative to each other.

17. Which of the following is an outcome of traditional systems for grading on the curve?

   a. The number of B's will exceed the number of A's.
   b. The number of A's will equal the number of D's.
   c. The least frequent grades will be B's and D's.
   d. The most frequent grade will be D.

18. Which of the following is true when a mastery grading system is used?

   a. The number of A's declines relative to a norm-referenced grading system.
   b. The most frequent grade earned is C.
   c. One student's grade has no bearing on another's.
   d. All of the above.

19. In assigning report card grades, it is recommended that

   a. grades should be communicated privately.
   b. only final achievement, not effort should be counted.
   c. written explanations of how a grade was derived be avoided.
   d. all of the above.

20. A teacher gives a very difficult test on which few students score above 80 percent. Which of the following is true?

a. A relative grading system will probably result in more A's than an absolute system.
b. Under a continuous progress system, approximately 20 percent of the students will receive A's.
c. A mastery grading system will probably result in more A's than a relative grading system.
d. Under a continuous progress grading system approximately 20 percent of the students will receive F's.

<u>APPLICATION:</u> Test Item Construction

Each of the following questions presents a potential test item containing a <u>major fault</u> peculiar to that type of item. Each item will be labeled as to type using the following key:

FI = Fill-in-the-blank
TF = True-False
SE = Short Essay

Describe the fault and briefly outline the most appropriate correction. (Assume that each item is content correct, relevant to course objectives, and appropriate to the grade levels and abilities of the students.)

A. (FI) John Glenn first orbited the earth in _____.
B. (FI) The United Nations Building is located in the city of ____ ____.
C. (TF) The best place to study is in a quiet room.
D. (SE) In constructing a test, what should be the relationship between the kinds of items used and the desired learning outcomes? Be sure to consider all possibilities.

Sections E and F each represent a <u>stem</u> of a multiple-choice item. Identify the fault in each.

E. Essay items:
F. Criterion-referenced tests, which have many uses in the field of education and in other areas, were first suggested by:

For sections G-H select which alternative set, 1 or 2, is more effective for the multiple-choice question shown. Then state the reason(s) for your choice.

G. Most authorities agree that sex education should begin at the age of

1. (a) 5 (b) 12 (c) 14 (d) 16
2. (a) 12 (b) 16 (c) 14 (d) 5

H. Which of the following represents what is meant by reforestration?
   1. (a) cutting (b) replanting (c) building (d) seeding
   2. (a) recutting (b) replanting (c) rebuilding (d) reseeding

<u>APPLICATION:</u> Personal Experiences in Testing Applications

Think about courses you have recently taken or observed. What types of tests were given? How were they employed? Characterize the "typical tests" given in relation to the following categories:

A. Formative vs. summative
B. Norm-referenced vs. criterion-referenced
C. Frequently given vs. infrequently given
D. Objective vs. essay

Overall, how do you feel about the validity and educational value of tests you have been given in your college courses?

<u>APPLICATION:</u> Grading Systems

Listed below are the test scores received (percent correct) by students in Ms. Wohl's algebra class. Assign different sets of <u>grades</u> to each using these absolute grading standards and relative grading standards:

<u>Absolute:</u> 90-100 (A); 80-89 (B); 70-79 (C); 60-69 (D); below 60 (F)

<u>Relative:</u> A=10% of students; B-25%; C=30%; D=25%; F=10%

Then answer the questions that appear below the test scores.

Student	Test Score
Frank	80
Marcos	93
Jamie	85
Will	98
Robin	82
Lorna	75
Corsica	85
Larry	97
Willis	87
Maureen	99
Elsa	100
Burt	100
Boris	98
Trevor	81
Sandra	84
Laurie	86
Anna	90
Francis	92
Alice	94
Ranjita	95

A. Which distribution yielded the higher grades?

B. Assuming that the test was valid and sufficiently challenging, which system would you prefer? Why?

C. The Honors Program at Mrs. Wohl's school has limited places for the best students. Which grading system might provide the best basis for nominations to that program? Explain.

D. Compare Frank's grades under both systems. What information does the grade provided by each convey to him regarding his performance?

APPLICATION: Effective Evaluation Practice

Read each of the descriptions below and present your views regarding the effectiveness of the evaluation practice used.

A. Ms. Davis tries to boost the morale of her less capable eighth-graders by grading their essay papers more leniently.

B. Mr. Jackson gives a "pop quiz" every week to stimulate continued involvement with the material. He evaluates the quizzes by awarding bonus points for good grades rather than by penalizing poor performances.

C. Ms. Bowles writes comments on the test papers she returns to students. Examples are "Good going!," "Nice improvement," "Grammar could be improved," etc.

D. Ms. Hogan, the psychology teacher at a community college, gives a 100-item true-false test as a mid-term.

E. Mr. Hernandez, the physical education teacher, grades his sixth-grade students on the curve in teaching them tennis fundamentals. Students in the top 10% in skills receive A; the next 20% B's; 40% C's; 20% D's; and the lowest 10% F's.

F. On her biology final, Mrs. Polazzi uses 10 multiple-choice questions, 10 fill-in-the-blank, 3 short essays, and 5 problem-solving items. She says that she likes to use a variety of item types rather than just one or two types.

COMPUTER EXERCISE: Testing and Grading

The EDUCATIONAL PSYCHOLOGY COMPUTER DISK for this text contains a program called GRADEBOOK. This program allows you to tabulate, graph, statistically describe, and assign letter grades to test scores that you provide or enter from existing files on the program disk. Thus, it functions as an applied tool to analyze test results and as a teaching tool to illustrate the principles of measurement and testing. The following are some exercises to guide your examination of the program.

a. Select the test file called CAKE TEST` and request a display of a frequency distribution, summary statistics, and histogram.

   1. What was the class mean?
   2. How did the class appear to do as a whole?

b. Then select the "Assign Grades" procedure and assign grades on CAKE TEST using each of the three grading systems.

   1. Criterion-referenced (absolute system)
   2. Normal Curve Based (relative system that assigns 10% F's and A's, 20% D's and B's, and 40% C's)
   3. Rectangular (relative system that assigns each letter grade to 20% of the students)

   How do the grades obtained by the different systems compare? Why are there more A's under the criterion-referenced system (unless your criteria were very high) than under the two relative grading systems?

c. Repeat the above exercises with the "Neither Hard nor Easy Test" and "Killer Test" files.

   How do results of the three grading systems change as test difficulty changes from low to moderate to high?

<u>ESSAY/DISCUSSION</u>

1. To effective teachers, evaluation means more than just assigning course grades. Identify and briefly discuss additional purposes that student evaluations can serve.

2. In what situations and for what purposes would classroom teachers be likely to use <u>formative</u> evaluations?

3. Differentiate between norm-referenced and criterion-referenced testing with regard to (a) principal uses, (b) content coverage, (c) item selection procedures, and (d) performance standards.

4. One of the important functions of achievement tests is to improve learning. Discuss strategies that teachers can use to increase the probability that this potential advantage will be realized.

5. Measurement specialists strongly concur that no single test item type is "best." Each is advantageous for certain types of testing uses. Describe the types of uses to which each of the following item types appears best-suited: (a) multiple-choice, (b) true-false, (c) fill-in-the-blank, (d) short essay, and (e) problem-solving.

6. Some educators have argued that report cards should not present letter grades, but instead should specify what the student can do

and cannot do. Present your views on this issue. Do letter grades serve a valuable purpose?

ANSWERS

Matching Warm-Ups

Quiz 1	Quiz 2	Quiz 3
a. 2 (474)	a. 2 (483)	a. 4 (496)
b. 1 (474)	b. 5 (484)	b. 3 (496)
c. 2 (474)	c. 3 (483)	c. 2 (493)
d. 2 (474)	d. 4 (484)	d. 1 (493)
e. 1 (474)	e. 1 (480)	

Key Terms

1. M (496)	8. G (479)
2. K (493)	9. L (496)
3. F (478)	10. D (474)
4. I (491)	11. C (474)
5. J (493)	12. H (480)
6. E (474)	13. A (468)
7. B (474)	

Completion Questions

1. feedback (468)
2. selection (471;473)
3. formative (474)
4. summative (474)
5. norm-referenced (474)
6. criterion-referenced (474)
7. incentive; feedback (475)
8. reliable (478)
9. table of specifications (479)
10. true-false (483)
11. fill-in-the-blank (483)
12. short essay items (484)
13. multiple-choice (480)
14. problem-solving (486-487)
15. relative (493)
16. absolute (493)
17. continuous progress (496)

Multiple-Choice

1.	b (469)	11.	c (491)
2.	b (469)	12.	c (483)
3.	a (474)	13.	d (484)
4.	d (474)	14.	b (492)
5.	a (475)	15.	d (494)
6.	c (475)	16.	b (496)
7.	b (478)	17.	a (494)
8.	b (478)	18.	c (496)
9.	c (483)	19.	a (496)
10.	d (482)	20.	a (493-494)

Application: Test Item Construction
(possible answers)

A. Too vague; in a spaceship? in a certain year?
B. The prompt lets us know that two words (such as New York) are needed; reduces effectiveness of item.
C. Answer is purely a matter of opinion.
D. Too complex for a short essay. Question needs to be more focused.
E. Stems should be as close to a complete sentence as possible. This one leaves too many words to be placed in distractors.
F. Stem should not include unneeded words such as, "which have many uses..."
G. 1 is better; numbers are in sequence and thus easier to consider.
H. 2 is better; all alternatives begin with "re," just as "reforestation" does.

15 Using and Interpreting Standardized Tests

CHAPTER OUTLINE

I. What are Standardized Tests?

II. Uses of Standardized Tests
  A. Selection and placement
  B. Diagnosis
  C. Evaluation

III. Types of Standardized Tests
  A. Aptitude tests
    1. General intelligence tests
    2. Multifactor aptitude tests
  B. Achievement tests
    1. Achievement batteries
    2. Diagnostic tests
    3. Specific subject achievement tests
    4. Criterion-referenced tests

IV. Interpreting Standardized Tests
  A. Types of scores
    1. Percentiles
    2. Grade equivalents
    3. Standard scores
  B. Validity, reliability, and bias
    1. Content validity
    2. Predictive validity
    3. Construct validity
    4. Reliability
    5. When is reliability adequate?

6. Criterion-referenced tests
7. Test bias

C. Teachers on teaching: Standardized tests

D. Theory into practice: Interpreting standardized test results

1. Class record forms
   a. Identification data
   b. List of students
   c. Form and level
   d. Scores
   e. Tests and subtests
   f. Individual performance information
   g. Quarter month interpolation
2. Individual test record
   a. Identification data
   b. Scores
   c. Confidence band
   d. Stanine bands
   e. Objectives scores
   f. Number of items not reached

V. Selecting Standardized Tests

A. Why are you testing in the first place?

1. Locating information on standardized tests
2. What to look for in choosing a standardized test
   a. Description of measured behavior
   b. Items per measured behavior
   c. Scope of measurement
   d. Reliability
   e. Validity
   f. Comparative data
   g. Ease of administration
   h. Absence of cultural bias

B. The uses of standardized tests in the schools

1. Contribution
2. Accountability

C. Problems and issues in standardized testing

1. Restricted test format
2. Truth-in-testing
3. Trends

Summary/Study Questions/Suggested Readings

CHAPTER OBJECTIVES

1. List three general purposes for which standardized tests are used in schools.
2. Describe the differences between aptitude tests and achievement tests, and between norm-referenced tests and criterion-referenced tests.

3. Interpret various types of scores used to report achievement on standardized tests, such as percentiles, grade equivalents, stanines, normal curve equivalents, and z-scores.
4. Assess the validity of a standardized test in terms of content, predictive ability, and quality relative to other tests.
5. Understand the issues involved in interpreting scores of students from lower-class or minority backgrounds, in using standardized tests to determine eligibility for high school graduation, and in informing people about tests and test results while ensuring high validity of tests.

MATCHING WARM-UPS

Match the numbers of the descriptions on the right to the corresponding items on the left. A given item from the right column may be used more than once or not at all.

Quiz 1: Types of Tests

_____	a. Achievement Battery	1. IQ test
_____	b. Aptitude Test	2. Used to guide remediation
_____	c. Diagnostic Test	3. Teacher-made test
_____	d. Specific Subject Test	4. California Achievement Test

Quiz 2: Types of Scores

_____	a. Percentile	1. The average score is 5.0
_____	b. Grade equivalents	2. An average 12-year-old might score about 7.0
_____	c. Normal curve equivalent	3. The average score is 0.0
_____	d. Stanine	4. Distribution averages 50 with a standard deviation of 21
_____	e. z score	5. Directly derived from class ranking

Quiz 3: Types of Validity

_____	a. Content validity	1. Whether tests can identify who will succeed in a certain endeavor
_____	b. Reliability	2. Whether tests measure the appropriate traits
_____	c. Construct validity	3. Whether tests provide accurate measurements
_____	d. Predictive validity	4. Whether tests cover what was taught

KEY TERMS

Fill in the blanks below with the letters identifying the following concepts. Each concept is used one time only.

A. Standardized tests
B. Norms
C. Aptitude tests
D. Intelligence
E. Multifactor aptitude battery
F. Achievement batteries
G. Cutoff scores
H. Derived scores
I. Percentile scores
J. Grade equivalent scores
K. Standard deviation
L. Stanines
M. Normal curve equivalent
N. z-scores
O. Validity
P. Content validity
Q. Predictive validity
R. Construct validity
S. Reliability

1. Standard scores having a mean of zero and a standard deviation of 1 are _____.

2. A test of ability to learn that provides a breakdown of specific skills is a(n) _____.

3. Test score standards that allow comparison of students' scores to a larger sample are called _____.

4. A measure of the "consistency" of test scores from one testing to the next is _____.

5. The percentages of students who fall below particular scores are represented by _____.

6. An index of the degree to which a test covers the specific material that was taught is _____.

7. A general term that refers to the degree to which a test is appropriate for its intended uses is _____.

8. Raw scores are converted into _____ to provide additional information about their meaning.

9. Commercially prepared tests designed to provide assessments under uniform conditions are generally referred to as _____.

10. Tests designed to forecast students' abilities to perform particular types of tasks are called _____.

11. Scores ranging from 1 to 9, with a mean of 5 and a standard deviation of 2 are _____.

12. The degree to which test scores relate to scores from measures of similar abilities is called _____.

13. Scores that relate performances to the level of achievement expected of students at specific grade levels are _____.

14. Scores that range from 1 to 99 with a mean of 50 are _____ scores.

15. A measure of the dispersion of scores is the _____.

16. A measure of the ability of a test to forecast future behavior is _____.

17. General aptitude for learning is measured by tests of _____.

18. Test score values used to determine whether mastery has been reached are _____.

19. Tests that provide a profile of the student's performance on a variety of specific skills are _____.

COMPLETION QUESTIONS

1. The SATs, ACTs, and other commercially prepared achievement or aptitude tests are examples of _____ tests.

2. Standards indicating what an average student will score on a test are called _____.

3. The three types of standardized tests commonly used in school settings are _____, _____, and _____.

4. _____ tests are designed to predict future performance, whereas _____ tests evaluate past performances.

5. The most common type of aptitude test is designed to measure _____.

6. The Otis-Lennon Mental Ability Test and the California Test of Mental Maturity are examples of _____ intelligence tests.

7. Students' specific strengths and weaknesses in different skills are identified on _____ tests.

8. Percentiles, grade equivalents, and normal curve equivalents are examples of _____ scores, used to increase the interpretability of raw scores.

9. Students scoring at the median would have a percentile rank of _____.

10. If a norming group beginning the seventh grade averaged 32 correct on a standardized test, the score of 32 would be established as a grade equivalent of _____.

11. A measure of the dispersion of scores is the _____.

12. A normal curve equivalent score can range from _____ to _____.

13. If a test measures what it is supposed to measure, it is considered to be _____.

14. In designing a new test of artistic ability, the test developer needs to demonstrate that it really measures that ability and not something else. The type of validity at issue is _____ validity.

15. A university uses applicants' high school grade point averages as a basis for selecting those with the best chances of succeeding. The assumption is that high school grades have _____ validity for that purpose.

16. The type of validity that might be evaluated, in part, with a careful examination of a table of specifications is _____ validity.

17. The highest possible reliability a test can have is _____.

18. Standardized tests designed to eliminate biases favoring middle-class students are called _____ tests.

19. The principal information source on published tests is the _____, edited by Buros.

20. The law requiring the results of tests to be released to students is the _____ law.

MULTIPLE-CHOICE

Select the best answer for each of the following items.

1. Which of the following types of standardized tests would be used to determine a student's math achievement relative to others?

    a. Diagnostic test
    b. Criterion-referenced test
    c. Norm-referenced test
    d. Aptitude test

2. The ACT and SAT exams that high school students take to gain admission to college are technically defined as _____ tests.

    a. achievement
    b. diagnostic
    c. aptitude
    d. criterion-referenced

3. Which type of standardized test would give information such as, "46% of eighth-graders in Western School District can divide fractions by whole numbers; whereas only 20% can divide fractions by fractions"?

   a. Diagnostic test
   b. Criterion-referenced test
   c. Norm-referenced test
   d. Aptitude test

4. An example of a group intelligence test is the

   a. Wechsler Intelligence Test for Children-Revised.
   b. Stanford-Binet.
   c. Otis-Lennon Mental Ability Tests.
   d. All of the above.

5. The landmark <u>Larry P. vs. Riles</u> case resulted in the ruling that in California

   a. parents of students given IQ tests must be given the results for their child.
   b. the validity of group IQ tests is too low to justify their use in psychological assessments.
   c. IQ tests cannot be used to classify individuals as retarded.
   d. teachers are allowed to administer individual IQ tests if properly trained.

6. Which of the following is <u>not</u> an example of a derived score?

   a. Martin's percentile rank on the test is 85.
   b. Brenda's test score was 92% correct.
   c. Marianne's grade equivalent in math is 8.3.
   d. Calvin's stanine score in reading is 5.

7. A third grader scores at 5.3 grade equivalents in reading. This can be interpreted to mean that he

   a. is ready for fifth-grade work.
   b. has a percentile rank of approximately 53.
   c. is performing over two-years above grade level.
   d. all of the above.

8. One class has a mean aptitude test score of 50, with a standard deviation of 5. Another has a mean of 51, with a standard deviation of 10. What can be concluded about these classes?

   a. The second class is significantly more capable.
   b. The first class is probably more difficult to teach.
   c. Scores in the second class are more varied.
   d. All of the above

9. Donnie's score of 75% correct on a standardized test surpasses 880 out of the 1000 students in the norming sample. His score is at the _____ percentile.

   a. 8.8th
   b. 75th
   c. 88th
   d. can't be determined without the norming sample mean.

10. The approximate percentage of scores in a normal distribution that falls between the mean and +1 SD from the mean is

   a. 34%
   b. 50%
   c. 68%
   d. 95%

11. A student scores exactly at the mean on an achievement test. Which of the following pairs of scores would represent her z-score and stanine score, respectively?

   a. 1 and 5
   b. 50 and 9
   c. 50 and 0
   d. 0 and 5

12. A teacher uses scores from a mathematics aptitude test to identify the students likely to have difficulty in his course. His main assumption is that the test has

   a. content validity.
   b. predictive validity.
   c. internal consistency reliability.
   d. construct validity.

13. A teacher constructs her test by carefully keeping track of the number of items that assess different types of learning from different parts of the course. Her main testing concern would appear to be

   a. content validity.
   b. predictive validity.
   c. internal consistency reliability.
   d. construct validity.

14. Test reliability is generally increased by

   a. making many items very easy.
   b. making many items very difficult.
   c. limiting the time available to take the test.
   d. adding more items to the test.

15. Research on culture-fair tests shows that they

    a. do not decrease the differential between minority and Anglo-American students.
    b. are culturally-biased.
    c. are not reliable.
    d. significantly decrease the differential between minority students and Anglo-American students.

16. A relatively high reliability index for an achievement test is

    a. 90
    b. .50
    c. .80
    d. 1.50

17. On which type of test would reliability be of relatively little importance?

    a. Creativity test
    b. Attitude survey
    c. Norm-referenced achievement test
    d. Criterion-referenced achievement test

18. Which of the following is considered a problem with current standardized testing?

    a. Teachers may vary the curriculum by "teaching to the test."
    b. Tests used have questionable validity.
    c. Tests used have low reliability.
    d. All of the above.

19. The group likely to react most negatively toward truth-in-testing laws is

    a. test publishers.
    b. teachers.
    c. students.
    d. parents.

20. The group likely to feel most threatened by the "accountability movement" is

    a. test publishers.
    b. teachers.
    c. students.
    d. parents.

APPLICATION: Interpreting Test Scores

In each of the descriptions below, the student concerned has received a derived test score. His/her parents, knowing that you have taken an educational psychology course, ask you to define the meaning. Provide a brief interpretation, indicating whether the student is about average, much higher than average, much lower, etc.

A. Rico received a stanine of 7 on a reading comprehension test.

B. Reba received a percentile rank of 67 in imagery ability.

C. Ann received a percentile rank of 30 in vocabulary.

D. Marcus, a tenth-grader, received a grade-equivalent of 9.3 in arithmetic reasoning.

E. Eileen received a z score of 0 in science.

F. Lorraine received a score of 510 on the verbal section of the SAT.

G. Paul received a NCE score of 90 in social studies.

H. Martin received a z score of -1.25 in language skills.

I. Eugene's IQ score was 95.

APPLICATION: Normal Curve Properties

Shown below is a normal curve measured in standard units (from -3 to +3). The approximate percentages of its area represented by some of the sections is provided. Fill in the missing percentages. Note: If you are aware of the fundamental normal curve properties, you do not need to recall any percentages. All the information needed to fill in the blanks is available below. (Assume that 100% of the area is represented from -3 to +3. Actually, an additional .24% is unaccounted for.) When you are done, answer the questions below the normal curve diagram.

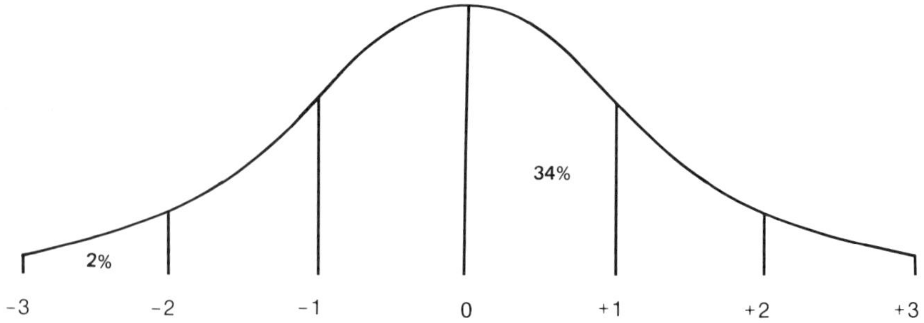

A. What is the raw score mean of the above distribution?

B. What specific raw score is most likely (or frequent) in the distribution?

C. Which raw score, 60 or 70, is more likely? Explain.

D. Which raw score is exactly as frequent as a raw score of 53?

APPLICATIONS: Establishing Validity

A friend of your says that she developed a new "scientific skills" test consisting of multiple-choice questions on knowledge and interpretive exercises on laboratory applications. She thinks it will be useful at the middle-school level in diagnosing difficulties, predicting success, assessing achievement, and other functions. You ask her about the test's validity, and she replies "validity? How do I determine that?"

This person obviously needs help. Describe in concrete terms the meaning of each of the following types of validity and what she would need to do to establish it.

A. Content
B. Construct
C. Predictive

APPLICATION: Locating Standardized Tests

Use the Mental Measurements Yearbook (Buros, 1978) at your library to identify one or more existing tests that measures each of the following:

A. Imagery ability
B. Mathematics anxiety
C. Self-esteem
D. Writing ability
E. Attitude toward school

COMPUTER EXERCISE: Standardized Tests

The EDUCATIONAL PSYCHOLOGY DISK for your text features a program called "Standardized Testing." It is directly linked to the chapter section, "Theory into Practice: Interpreting Standardized Test Results." The program gives you practice at interpreting test results, as recorded on the individual and group records forms presented in the textbook. After you respond, it provides feedback on your answer and indicates the correct interpretation.

If you have a copy of the disk, try the two quizzes and see how you do. A score of 80% on each is considered "mastery."

ESSAY/DISCUSSION

1. Define "standardized test" and describe three different common applications of such tests.

2. A teacher says to you "These statistics like percentile ranks and stanines get me all confused. Why don't they just report percent correct scores and leave it at that?" What would be your reply? Are derived scores valuable or do they just confuse and complicate things? Briefly differentiate between raw score, derived score, and standard score, and give examples of each.

3. The IQ controversy has created considerable interest in developing "culture-fair" tests that do not discriminate against minority and lower-class children. What has been the experiences with these tests? Have they accomplished their intended purpose? In your opinion, can there be a truly "culture-fair" test? Explain.

4. Fundamental criteria for a test to be effective are that it is both valid and reliable. Define and distinguish between validity and reliability. Is it necessary for a test to be valid to be reliable? Is it necessary for a test to be reliable to be valid? Explain.

5. "Truth in Testing" laws have provoked mixed reactions among different groups. Describe what such laws involve, and discuss their implications from the perspective of the test developer and the consumer.

ANSWERS

Matching Warm-Ups

Quiz 1	Quiz 2	Quiz 3
a. 4 (504)	a. 5 (507)	a. 4 (510)
b. 1 (502)	b. 2 (507)	b. 3 (513)
c. 2 (505)	c. 4 (509)	c. 2 (512)
d. 3 (505)	d. 1 (509)	d. 1 (511)
	e. 3 (509)	

Key Terms

1. N (509)	7. O (510)	13. J (507)
2. E (504)	8. H (506)	14. M (509)
3. B (500)	9. A (500)	15. K (508)
4. S (513)	10. C (501)	16. Q (511)
5. I (507)	11. L (509)	17. D (503)
6. P (510)	12. R (512)	18. G (506)
		19. F (504)

Completion Questions

1. standardized (500)
2. norms (500)
3. aptitude tests; norm-referenced achievement tests; criterion-referenced achievement tests (502)
4. aptitude; achievement (502)
5. intelligence (503)
6. group (503)
7. diagnostic (505)
8. derived (506)
9. 50 (507)
10. 7.0 (507)
11. standard deviation (509)
12. 1; 99 (509)
13. valid (510)
14. construct (512)
15. predictive (511)
16. content (510)
17. 1.00 (513)
18. culture-fair (516)
19. Mental Measurements Yearbook (519)
20. Truth in Testing (523)

Multiple-Choice

1. c (503)
2. c (502)
3. b (503)
4. c (503)
5. c (504)
6. b (506-509)
7. c (507)
8. c (509)
9. c (507)
10. a (509)
11. d (509)
12. b (512)
13. a (510)
14. d (513)
15. a (516)
16. c (513)
17. d (514)
18. a (523)
19. a (523)
20. b (523)

Application: Interpreting Test Scores

a. Higher than average (509)
b. Higher than average (507)
c. Lower than average (507)
d. Slightly lower than average (509)
e. Average (509)
f. Close to average (508)
g. Much higher than average (509)
h. Much lower than average (509)
i. Close to average (508)